East Saxon Heritage

East Saxon Heritage
An Essex Gazetteer

STEPHEN PEWSEY
and
ANDREW BROOKS

Photographs by
MARK GALLOWAY

ALAN SUTTON

First published in the United Kingdom in 1993 by
Alan Sutton Publishing Limited
Phoenix Mill · Far Thrupp · Stroud · Gloucestershire

First published in the United States of America in 1993 by
Alan Sutton Publishing Inc.
83 Washington Street · Dover · NH 03820

British Library Cataloguing in Publication Data

Pewsey, Stephen
　East Saxon Heritage: Essex Gazetteer
　I. Title II. Brooks, Andrew
　936

　ISBN 0–7509–0290–6

Library of Congress Cataloging in Publication Data applied for

In Memory of Our Mothers

Typeset in 11/13.
Typesetting and origination by
Alan Sutton Publishing Limited.
Printed in Great Britain by
The Bath Press, Avon.

CONTENTS

Abbreviations vi

Introduction

The East Saxon Legacy vii

An Outline of East Saxon History ix

Gazetteer

Sites in Essex 1

Sites in Other Counties 95

References and Notes 113

Bibliography 122

ABBREVIATIONS

The following abbreviations are used in the Gazetteer:

DB   Domesday Book

ASC   *Anglo Saxon Chronicle*. Unless otherwise stated in the references and notes, Version E (The Laud (Peterborough) Chronicle: Bodleian MS. Laud 636) is used throughout

*   The use of * before a word is standard etymological practice to indicate a hypothetically reconstructed place-name based on known rules, the later form of the name, and parallels. Because of the rules applying to sound changes, etymologists are reasonably certain about the accuracy of their reconstruction, even though the name itself is not actually attested from charters or any other early literary source.

INTRODUCTION

The East Saxon Legacy

In the dignified and impressive Council Chamber of Essex County Hall, the painted panels and maps depicting great events in Essex history are surmounted by a frieze bearing the names of the Saxon kings of Essex. More than a thousand years separate us from these names that look down on our modern, elected, leaders and administrators; but are they mere names, or does anything remain of their legacy? Surprisingly enough, there are many physical remains of Saxon Essex, that long and formative span of history from the fifth century to 1066. Indeed, though the East Saxon kingdom was never of more than local importance, we are fortunate that the surviving monuments include some of the country's greatest treasures from that age.

Overlooking the Thames stands the bleak hillside of Mucking, home to some of the first Anglo-Saxon settlers in Britain, while at Waltham Abbey lies the tomb of the last Anglo-Saxon king of England. At Bradwell-on-Sea the stone chapel of St Cedd has defied the wind and waves for over a millennium. On the other side of the county in a green nook lies the unique wooden Saxon church of Greensted. The long wars with the Vikings are reflected in a scatter of battle sites and fortified camps across the county. There are little Saxon churches too, lying like hidden jewels in the lanes of deepest Essex – Chickney, Strethall, and many more incorporating Saxon work. Ecclesiastical work naturally predominates in any list of survivals from the Saxon age, but how many know that 'the oldest house in England' stands in Essex, at Widdington?

Furthermore, the heritage of the East Saxons survives not only in buildings. Beautiful examples of their craftsmanship can be seen in the county's museums. The finest gem- and metal-craft, like the Broomfield Treasure, has a place in the British Museum alongside, and worthy of comparison with, the finds from Sutton Hoo. In the written word, the thoughts of Saxon men ring down the ages in the epic poem celebrating the Battle of Maldon, a literary masterpiece that ranks with the greatest of works in Old English.

Such is the diversity of the East Saxon legacy. It is all the more surprising, therefore, to find that the richness of this heritage has never before been brought together in a single work, and that is why we have drawn up this guidebook. We live in an age when the value of our past is being increasingly recognized, yet the rate of destruction continues apace. In a developing county like Essex, the archaeologist's trowel is often only a few minutes in front of the builder's bulldozer. However, we hope that this book will draw attention to the fact that much still survives to remind us of the county's Saxon origin.

Of course, such a book can never be comprehensive, nor should it aim to be. There is an element of selection, particularly in the later, eleventh-century churches. New archaeological discoveries are coming to light all the time, some of which alter our views on the politics or daily life of the past. In that sense, a guidebook such as this is out of date as soon as it is written. Nevertheless, the great majority of standing Saxon remains in Essex from AD 400 to 1066 have been gathered together in this gazetteer, together with an introduction that outlines the creation, politics, and decline of the East Saxon kingdom. Much remains obscure about the history of the East Saxons, but within these constraints we have tried to present plausible models rather than discuss in detail every possible nuance and by-way; this has been done elsewhere with exemplary and admirable clarity.[1]

The area covered includes the whole of the 'ancient county' of Essex, comprising the modern administrative county and metropolitan Essex, now the five London Boroughs of Barking & Dagenham, Havering, Newham, Redbridge, and Waltham Forest. The whole of London, Middlesex and much of Hertfordshire was part of the East Saxon kingdom until the end of the seventh century – indeed London was the capital of Essex during that time – and remains relating to that period in these areas have therefore also been included, although in practice they consist only of sites in the City of London. These have been covered in a separate section at the end of the guide together with a few other sites of interest outside the county.

This book is intended to appeal to the layman as well as the enthusiast, and no specialist archaeological or architectural knowlege is assumed or required. All the entries include directions and access notes. In this age of the car, there is an inevitable bias towards the driver, but we have tried to incorporate guidance for walkers and rail travellers wherever possible. Last but by no means least, Essex is fortunate in possessing an extensive rural bus network, with many special offers and weekend services, particularly in the summer months. Because of changing schedules, it has not been possible to include relevant bus routes, but comprehensive timetables, maps and details of family saver, rambler and Sunday saver tickets are available from the Public Transport and Tourism Sections of Essex County Council Planning Department, Globe House, New Street, Chelmsford (telephone 0245 352232).

The seven Ordnance Survey Landranger Series maps (1:50,000) covering Essex (nos. 154, 155, 167, 168, 169, 177, 178) are invaluable whatever the form of transport, as are the Ordnance Survey East Essex and West Essex Street Atlases. General information for the visitor is available from the efficient new Essex Tourist Information Centre at the new County Hall Extension, Market Street, Chelmsford (0245–283400), open Monday to Friday 9.30 a.m. to 5.30 p.m. and Saturday 9.30 a.m. to 4.00 p.m.

Some of the sites featured in the guide are on private property; the visitor is asked to respect private land and obtain permission before approaching the site. Many churches have to be kept locked in these days of theft and wanton vandalism. We have highlighted those churches which are kept locked, and tried to give a contact telephone number for access. Please be reasonable about times, etc. when requesting access. All sites, but particularly churches, should be treated with care when visited; many rural parishes have difficulty maintaining the fabric of the churches in their care, so donations are always welcomed.

For those not familiar with our Saxon history we hope that this book will serve as an introduction which shows that everyone in Essex lives close to some visible remains of those far-off days, while for old friends of the county we hope you will find one or two surprises as well as pleasure through re-acquaintance with our cherished past.

An Outline of East Saxon History

In AD 410 the Roman government of Britain was ended as the central authorities were unable to maintain control of this distant island any longer in the face of so many pressing problems nearer home. Roman Britain had been part of the Empire for 350 years and was no doubt well Romanized. The area we now call Essex was then part of the

The early Kingdom of Essex and its neighbours

civitas or canton of the *Trinovantes*, a tribe who before the Roman occupation had controlled much of southern Britain from their capital at Colchester. Colchester, or *Camulodunum*, remained an important city for the Romans. Chelmsford was *Caesaromagus*. There were smaller towns too, such as *Canonium*, at Kelvedon, and *Durolitum*, near Chigwell, as well as towns whose Roman names were unknown, such as Great Chesterford, Braintree and Heybridge. Rural settlement may have changed little since the Iron Age, though there was a scatter of Romanized farmsteads and villas; however, these were not so large or luxurious as those found elsewhere in Britain. Some areas, such as Dengie and the Thurrock peninsula, were systematically adapted to a large-scale farming and occupation pattern; the rectilinear landscape this produced can still be traced in field boundaries and road alignments today.

Yet within a generation or two the Roman-style economy had vanished, cities were abandoned or in sharp decline, and *Romanitas* was quickly being replaced with loyalty to a new breed of native British chieftain and lifestyle. New states emerged, though often the new leaders liked titles redolent of imperial power. The chief remaining link with Rome was Christianity. From the middle of the fifth century Saxons and other Germanic mercenaries, long stationed in Britain, were reinforced by large numbers of new Germanic settlers and they began seizing territory. This process soon grew and the lands conquered by Saxons were made into kingdoms, which gradually overwhelmed the British states.

Unfortunately the exact nature of this conquest is obscure because of the very few literary sources we have for the fifth and sixth centuries. For both British and Saxon accounts we often must rely on annals compiled much later, whose accuracy it is hard to assess. However, the general trend of the story is clear. In the first half of the fifth century the British leaders struggled to maintain a civic lifestyle against increasing odds.[2] Some town-life continued, though it hardly flourished. More Germanic peoples were arriving all the time; once the legions had withdrawn they may have been the only effective defence against even greater incursions, which came from Ireland and the Picts as well as the Continent. One British leader, Vortigern, was remembered for inviting Hengest and Horsa, Germanic warrior princes, from across the North Sea.[3]

It was these two who traditionally began the process of Saxon conquest. Hengest took the crown in Kent, and the second half of the fifth century was remembered by the Saxons for the establishment of more kingdoms. Under pressure, British resistance seems to have become more determined however. The fightback was traditionally led by Ambrosius Aurelianus,[4] who may have claimed noble Roman descent, and, at the end of the fifth century and in the early sixth, by Arthur. His victories over the Saxons were traditionally so overwhelming that they were forced back to an enclave in the south-east, where they were unable to expand for a generation. As might be expected, Anglo-Saxon records present a rather different picture; one of steady consolidation and advancement. Literary sources are largely silent as to the fate of Essex, though a passage in the early ninth-century compilation known as *Historia Brittonum* (*The History of the Britons*) claims that after Hengest and his followers had treacherously slain all the British leaders and captured Vortigern, Vortigern ceded Essex, Sussex and Middlesex to Hengest in exchange for his life.[5] Evidence of British resistance in Essex has been suggested through place-name study (see entry for Ambresbury Banks), but this must be regarded as very dubious.

Archaeological evidence indicates early Saxon settlement in many parts of Essex, including Mucking and Colchester (see entries below), Barling, Heybridge, and Bulmer, all riverside sites. Other possible early settlement sites stick mainly to coastal or riverine locations;[6] more are gradually coming to light as development pressure on the county increases and archaeological techniques improve.

There are few *archaeological* signs of sub-Roman continuity, although topographical evidence suggests that a discrete area around Great Chesterford and Saffron Walden remained a British enclave for some time (see entry for Saffron Walden). The Saxon population in Essex must have been a very small minority of the population for a considerable time[7] after the *Adventus Saxonum*, that is to say, the period around the mid-fifth century when the Saxons first established kingdoms and began conquering British territory. However, in Essex, 'there is hardly any evidence of violence or destruction',[8] rather 'growing evidence for gradual and peaceful Saxon infiltration and the slow collapse of the Romano-British way of life'.[9]

The kingdom of the East Saxons was founded in great obscurity. How was the Roman *civitas* of the *Trinovantes* transformed into the Saxon kingdom of Essex? With virtually no documentary or archaeological evidence to cast light on the politics of fifth- and sixth-century Essex, the enigma remains unsolved. However, a number of plausible models can be proposed.

The most drastic model has Essex transmuting directly into a Saxon kingdom from sub-Roman *Trinovantia*.[10] This sort of lock, stock and barrel take-over has parallels elsewhere in England,[11] although the apparently late emergence of East Saxon kingship would then be difficult to explain. More plausible and better evidenced is the suggestion that a number of smaller proto-kingdoms developed within what is now Essex, which then coalesced to form the East Saxon kingdom.[12] These statelets could have coalesced 'internally', that is to say, with the emergence of a strong central leader or dynasty, or 'externally', that is to say, a foreign leader imposed, or native leader raised up by some neighbouring paramount power. In the case of Essex, Kent is likely to have been that power, and there was certainly Kentish intervention in sixth- and seventh-century East Saxon royal affairs (see below).

As in all other Anglo-Saxon kingdoms there is certainly evidence of distinct regions within Essex, out of which the kingdom arose. They can be deduced from etymological and topographical evidence. The earliest organized blocs of settlement are represented by the place-name element *ge–, meaning district (paralleled in the modern German *gau*). These *ge– were known in Latin as *regiones*; the *regio* of the *Deningei* (Dengie) is referred to in an eighth-century charter. Other such districts were Vange (derived from *fenn ge* meaning 'fen district') in the Thurrock peninsula, and *Gegingas* (meaning 'the dwellers in the district'), an extensive district in the Wid Valley south-west of Chelmsford. In both Dengie and Thurrock a rectilinear Roman field and road pattern survived largely intact, perhaps because of the autonomy of such areas in the post-Roman and early Saxon periods.[13] There is a fuller discussion of the Dengie, *Gegingas* and Vange areas under the entries for Danbury, Buttsbury, and Corringham respectively.

Another, probably secondary, wave of settlement is represented in place-names ending in –ingas. Several *ingas* districts can be identified in Essex, at *Berecingas* (Barking, see separate entry), *Eppingas* (Epping), *Haeferingas* (Havering) and *Hrothingas* (Roding – see entry for Beauchamp Roding). Each of these districts provides a mix of land types, is well watered, and straddles a Roman road.[14] Both the *ge– and the –ingas regions should perhaps be thought of like the Irish *tuath*, a kindred or tribe.[15] Royal estates are also a clue to early land units; such *villae regales* are known at Waltham Abbey (see discussion under entry for Waltham Abbey) and Bonhunt[16] in the Great Chesterford/Saffron Walden district discussed above. A royal estate also existed at Havering. There was probably another in central Essex, where we find the adjacent parishes of Broomfield, where there was a sixth-century East Saxon royal burial (see entry for Broomfield), Writtle, where there was a post-Conquest royal hunting lodge, and Great and Little Waltham, which place-name is thought likely to indicate an early royal estate.[17] It has also been suggested[18] that hundreds, established as local administration units in the tenth century,[19] often reflect earlier land units. Rochford and Tendring Hundreds, with their geographical cohesiveness, may be examples of this.

In the Middle Saxon area there were similar tribal groupings; *Beningas, Brahingas, Gedingdas, Gillingas, Gumeningas, Haemele, Lullingas, Mimmas, Staeningas*, and *Wixan*.[20] It is unclear whether Middlesex was East Saxon from the start (see discussion under Sites in Other Counties, London), or whether it was added to the kingdom by Kentish overlords. The name Middlesex does not occur until the eighth century,[21] and reflects Mercian dominion – they are likely to have invented the term when they annexed the Middlesex area from Essex.[22]

The East Saxon kingdom finally emerged during the sixth century, though historical sources disagree as to the name of the first king. Some state that it was Sledd,[23] who reigned during the second half of the sixth century, while others claim that his father, who was named either Aescwine or Erkenwine, was the first ruler. Aescwine/Erkenwine had a name which may indicate a Kentish origin.[24] Essex certainly owed suzerainty to Kent in the late sixth and early seventh centuries, and his name may either be an interpolation recalling a period of Kentish rule, or a genuine memory of a sub-king planted by the Kentish kings north of the Thames in order to secure rule there. Aescwine/Erkenwine's name is one of the very few which does not begin with the letter S, which was such a characteristic feature of the names of the kings of Essex.

The next name on the regnal list is that of Sledd, the first man we can say with certainty to reign as king of Essex. His accession is dated by some sources to AD 587. Sledd married Ricula, sister of King Ethelbert of Kent. Ethelbert was *bretwalda* or overlord of the southern English, and made a series of useful dynastic alliances by marriage to cement this control. The village of Rickling in north-west Essex derives its name from Ricula, although not necessarily the Ricula who was Sledd's wife. We can assume the continuation of Kentish overlordship during Sledd's reign; the date of his death is unknown but his son Saberht was certainly ruling by 604, when Bede records the conversion of the East Saxons.[25] In that year Saberht's uncle, Ethelbert of Kent, had St Paul's Cathedral built and Mellitus installed as first bishop of the East Saxons.

Little is known about the pagan beliefs held by the East Saxons before their conversion. The names of the pantheon of gods are known; Woden and Thunor have left their mark on East Saxon place-names (see entries for Thundersley and Thurstable). Places of pagan worship are also known in Essex (see entry for Harrowdown), and some of their temples or sacred places survived the conversion to Christianity to become churches.[26] Sacred pagan stones – usually glacial boulders or strange-looking pudding-stones – were often incorporated into the fabric of churches, as at Ingatestone and Broomfield (see entries below). Certain springs and wells were also regarded as holy, and this water veneration also passed into passed into Christianity.[27] Traditionally the various dynasties of the Anglo-Saxon kingdoms traced their descent from Woden, but the kings of Essex alone claimed descent from Seaxnet (meaning 'need of the Saxons'), who was probably originally the 'national' god of the

Saxons.[28] This unique claim emphasizes the 'Saxon-ness' of the East Saxon kings, and also marks out a separate religious and royal identity for the East Saxons.

By the early seventh century the East Saxon kingdom included not only Essex but all of Middlesex and much of southern and eastern Hertfordshire, as is indicated by the early boundaries of the diocese of London. The diocese would naturally have been coterminous with the kingdom. Charters showing royal grants of land can also indicate which areas were within the East Saxon kingdom; for instance, the late seventh-century King Offa granted land at *pago Haemele* (modern Hemel Hempstead). Braughing too, in present-day Hertfordshire, was the subject of a grant,[29] but the Hitchin area seems to have been outside the kingdom. *Hicce* was still listed separately from Essex in the Tribal Hidage, a late seventh-century Mercian document compiled for assessment of tribute, and seems to have survived long enough for the preservation of an eponymous hero-legend. The tale of Tom Hickathrift (meaning 'prosperity of the *Hicce*') was known not only in Hertfordshire but also in Cambridgeshire and Norfolk[30] as well as north-west Essex;[31] versions of the tale were still being published in the nineteenth century.

To the west the boundary was probably the Colne, still a county boundary. The relationship of the St Alban's area with Essex is unclear, but north-western Hertfordshire and the slopes of the Chilterns were never part of Essex. This area was part of the autonomous *Cilternsaete* in the seventh century, a well-defined upland that may have been an independent British kingdom, known as *Calchvynydd*, until as late as the sixth century.[32]

The relationship of Surrey to Essex is problematic. Its name (meaning 'the southern region') implies that it was once part of a larger northern region encompassing both Middlesex and Surrey. Surrey lay within the diocese of the bishop of London (and Essex) in the seventh century, though perhaps as early as 705x706 it had been transferred to Winchester.[33] Surrey had long been an area of conflict between Kentish and West Saxon kings, so although the province was East Saxon by implication, it is difficult to prove historically, as it would have been detached early. St Erkenwald founded both Chertsey and Barking Abbeys in the 660s; these may have been at either end of the original Surrey/Middlesex 'circum-metropolitan' region.

King Saberht is likely to have had London as his capital in the early seventh century. A royal precinct is believed to have existed within the former Roman fort at Cripplegate (see entry under Sites in Other

Counties, City of London), with perhaps an ecclesiastical precinct to the south around the earliest St Paul's (which would have been a timber building). To the west along The Strand lay the burgeoning trading centre of *Lundenwic*, a market and manufacturing area outside the city walls (see Introduction to London entry). Saberht died in 616 or 617, leaving three sons to reign as joint kings. By tradition, Saberht's body was at some stage interred in Westminster Abbey, where the tomb can still be seen today (see entry under Sites in Other Counties, City of London).

Of Saberht's sons, the names of only two are known for certain; they were Seaxred and Saeward. The third son may have been Seaxbald.[34] Unlike their father, the three sons were resolutely pagan and had expelled Mellitus by 618. Kentish influence in Essex declined after the death of Ethelbert in 616, and the new English *bretwalda* or overlord was Raedwald, king of East Anglia. Under Raedwald's leadership, a spectacular east-country school of craftsmanship flourished, and a skilful foreign policy was pursued. The Sutton Hoo burial, generally accepted as that of Raedwald,[35] comprised a sumptuous assemblage of personal adornments befitting an overking. Many of the Sutton Hoo items find close stylistic parallels with grave goods from the Broomfield burial (see entry for Broomfield), from the Taplow mound in Buckinghamshire, and a rich female burial at Forest Gate,[36] and they are probably all the work of a single brilliant but short-lived metal- and jewellery-working school, perhaps based at the East Anglian royal court at Rendlesham.

The East Saxon royal family seems thus to have been drawn into the East Anglian cultural sphere, as well as its political sphere; the Broomfield burial must have been of someone of princely if not royal status, although it is impossible to know whose burial it represents.

Taplow means 'the burial-mound of Taeppa', and it has been suggested[37] that Taeppa was a client king of Raedwald in the early seventh century, installed in newly conquered territory to the west of Essex, in what is now south Buckinghamshire.

In about 623 the three kings of Essex were killed fighting the West Saxons. Bede saw this as divine retribution for their paganism,[38] but the reason for the battle is likely to have been a frontier dispute either in Surrey[39] or in the area of Taeppa's kingdom, with the East Saxon kings perhaps fighting as Raedwald's proxies.

Raedwald's death occurred at about the same time, and the position of *bretwalda* passed to Edwin of Northumbria. The East Saxon throne passed to Sigeberht, nicknamed *Parvus* (meaning 'small') by Bede to distinguish him from his successor Sigeberht *Sanctus*. Little is known about Sigeberht *Parvus* except that, like his predecessors, he remained a pagan.

The relationship of the two Sigeberhts, *Parvus* and *Sanctus*, to the surviving genealogical tables is problematic;[40] only one Sigeberht is in the right chronological position, as son of Saeward. This was probably Sigeberht *Sanctus*, and if so, Sigeberht *Parvus* was from another line, perhaps son of Seaxa, Saberht's brother.

It is very curious that at the precise time when the two Sigeberhts were ruling successively in Essex, a mysterious Sigeberht was also on the throne in East Anglia. He acceded in about 630 after a period of chaos in that kingdom. He apparently reigned jointly with one Ecgric, also a mysterious figure. A Christian, Sigeberht of East Anglia abdicated at an unknown date and retired to a monastery, only to be forcibly removed from it subsequently in order to assist Ecgric in his war against the Mercians. He was then killed in the battle that followed. Sigeberht, ostensibly brother of the previous king, stands out very starkly against the other names in the East Anglian king-list, which mostly alliterate with R– or E–. It is hard to dismiss as coincidence concurrent Sigeberhts in neighbouring kingdoms. If they were one and the same person, however, Bede would surely have mentioned the fact. Yet in any other circumstance, the 'case of the two Sigeberhts' would be taken as indicating confused memories of East Saxon intervention in East Anglia.

The date of Sigeberht *Parvus'* death is unknown, though Sigeberht *Sanctus* was ruling by 653. This was the approximate date of his conversion to Christianity; he was baptized at the royal court of the Northumbrian King Oswiu, to whom Sigeberht was friend and frequent visitor. Oswiu sent St Cedd to Essex to begin again the work of converting Essex, and this new bishop of the East Saxons established several churches, notably at *Ythancaestir* (Bradwell-on-Sea) and at *Tilaburg* (East Tilbury) (see entries below), from which priests were ordained and the faith spread. Though imperilled, it was never to die out again.

Sigeberht *Sanctus* was murdered by two brothers, his own kinsmen, unable to bear his piety; the date of his death is also unknown. It is possible that the succeeding kings, Swithhelm and Swithfrith, were brothers, and if so, these may have been the murderers.[41] Bede calls Swithhelm 'son of Seaxbald', who, as we have seen above, may have been the third son of Saberht. Bede does not, however, mention Swithfrith, who is known only from a Barking

Abbey schedule of grants, as a donor of land. Swithhelm was baptized at Rendlesham, the East Anglia royal estate near Sutton Hoo, and by tradition he was buried there too.[42] Swithhelm was dead by 664; the date of Swithfrith's death is not known, though it may have been before Swithhelm as Bede regards the accession of Saebbi and Sigehere as following Swithhelm's death.

Through Bede and surviving charters we know much about the reign of Saebbi and Sigehere. In about 665 a serious plague caused Sigehere to abandon Christianity, though Saebbi remained faithful 'with all his people'.[43] The Mercian king sent a missionary bishop to Essex as soon as he learnt that 'part of the province' had apostatized. This implies that the two kings – and, as we have seen, multiple kingship was a feature of East Saxon monarchy – ruled separate areas. Saebbi is explicitly stated to have lived in London[44] so he may have ruled the Middlesex area, while Sigehere ruled Essex 'proper'.

Sigehere was at any rate reconverted to the faith. Later in his reign he was traditionally associated with Osyth, saint and martyr. After his marriage to her he granted land for her to found a monastery at Cicc, now St Osyth, where she was later beheaded by priates (see entry for St Osyth). Although his death is placed in 683 by some historical sources, this seems to be a mistake for he is found in the later 680s conquering part of Kent, probably the western half[45] during a period of disruption there. His date of death is more likely to be about 688.

Saebbi reigned for thirty years (probably dying in about 693) and was a man renowned for his piety, whose only desire was to retire to a monastery. He has been associated with the building of The Strood causeway across to Mersea Island (see entry for West Mersea), and miracles attended his death and burial. By tradition he was interred in St Paul's Cathedral (see entry under Sites in Other Counties, City of London). St Erkenwald, the founder of Barking Abbey, was his bishop for much of his reign. Also of some importance and described as Saebbi's 'kin' in a charter was Oethelred, who granted land to Barking in 686x688, though his exact status is unclear.

Saebbi was succeeded by a committee of kings; in Kent, his son Swaefheard had ruled from about 688–94. In Essex his other two sons Sigeheard and Swaefred reigned, together with Sigehere's saintly son Offa. Offa seems to have been of lesser status than the other two, and he abdicated in 709 when he departed with Cenred, king of Mercia, on a pilgrimage to Rome. His name, the only one in the East Saxon regnal list not S-alliterative, and his pilgrimage companion, indicates the increasing dependency of Essex on Mercia. Mercian overlordship was to strengthen and continue in Essex until the ninth-century West Saxon conquest, with a consequent reduction in the status of the East Saxon kings.

Sigeheard and Swaefred were succeeded by Selered and Swaefberht. Selered was a very distant relative of the previously reigning kings and Swaefberht's ancestry is unknown. In general, much less is known of eighth-century East Saxon kings than of the previous century. Swaefberht died in 738 and Selered in 746; according to the *Anglo-Saxon Chronicle* he was slain, but the circumstances are unknown. They were succeeded by Swithred, the first sole ruler for some time. The date of his death is unknown, but he was succeeded by a distant relative, Sigeric. The *Anglo-Saxon Chronicle* records his departure for Rome (and therefore presumably his abdication) in 798, and he was succeeded by Sigered. He was one of a group of kings who submitted to the West Saxons following the Battle of *Ellendun*, at which the Mercians were decisively defeated by the West Saxon army.

Unlike the Mercians the West Saxons allowed no sub-kings in tributary territories, so Sigered is sometimes considered to be the last East Saxon king. However, after 827 a further king is recorded in a charter; this was Sigeric (II). His parentage is unknown, though he was likely to have been closely related to his predecessors. How long he reigned, or indeed how he did manage to reign in the face of West Saxon hegemony, is unknown, but his name marks the end of the independent kingdom of Essex.

The ninth century was overshadowed by the menace of the Vikings, whose furious assaults on these islands almost overwhelmed the only power able to resist, that of Wessex. When the Great Army struck in 865 Essex was overrun and was to remain in Viking hands until 912. Even then the reconquest was not completed until 917. During the occupation Essex had been an important base for raiding deeper into England, and the fortified camps set up by the Vikings at East Mersea, South Benfleet, and South Shoebury were an important element in their strategy (see separate entries on these locations). The reconquest was a painstaking affair, involving the establishment of fortress *burhs* at Witham and Maldon, and finally the storming of Colchester (see separate entries below).

Towards the end of the tenth century there were renewed Viking attacks, which continued for a generation until Cnut was finally able to seize the whole kingdom in 1016. Two of the key battles of this Danish campaign were fought in Essex. One was at Maldon in 991 where the heroic bravery and defeat of the English warriors was the subject of an outstanding epic poem, one of the finest written in Anglo-Saxon (see entry for Maldon). The other was at *Assandun* where Edmund Ironside was defeated by Cnut's forces after treachery on the part of some of his own men (see entry for Ashingdon).

England remained in Danish hands until 1042 when Edward the Confessor came to the throne and there was a final brief flowering of Anglo-Saxon culture. His successor, the ill-starred Harold II, had close connections with Essex (see entry for Waltham Abbey), and at the Battle of Hastings the English battle-cry was 'Holy Cross!' (of Waltham). This last Anglo-Saxon king was buried in Essex at Waltham Abbey, and with his death a distinctive and formative era in English history ended.

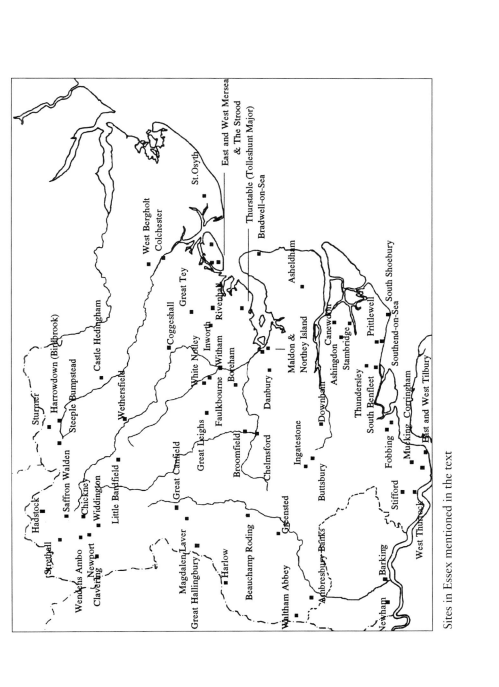

Sites in Essex mentioned in the text

GAZETTEER

SITES IN ESSEX

Ambresbury Banks
Earliest known form of name: **Amesbury** 1670[46]
Derivation: see below

This ancient earthwork, which occupies the highest point in Epping Forest, was first built in the fifth century BC[47] and is still an impressive sight today. The Amesbury/Ambresbury name does not occur until 1670; the only known earlier name is *castrum de Eppynghatthe*, which occurs in 1299.[48] Some authorities have, however, assumed that the Ambresbury name is ancient, and an intriguing but decidely unproven theory has been developed around the name.

There is a scattering of place-names across southern England containing the element *Ambros–*. Essex has the greatest concentration of these *Ambros–* names, and it has been suggested[49] that these form part of late fifth-century British defence against Saxon invasion. One of the traditional leaders of the British resistance to the Saxons was Ambrosius Aurelianus, and it has been proposed that troops raised under his banner were known as *Ambrosiaci*. If they existed, these would have been cavalry units, and *Ambros—* place-names could mark their various posting stations and garrisons. Surviving *Ambros—* names in Essex form a rough arc mainly following high ground from Walthamstow, through Ambresbury and round towards the Blackwater Estuary.

Ambresbury is the only one of these sites known to have been fortified, though repeated excavation has failed to find any post-Roman refortification of the camp.[50] The theory must, therefore, be treated with extreme caution, and a more likely explanation is that the place-names come from a Saxon personal name *Æmbre*.[51] But anyone wandering around the haunting ramparts today could be forgiven for imagining warriors of far-off days selecting these fortifications as the place for a last-ditch stand.

Location: Ambresbury Banks are beside the B1393 (Epping High Road) about 2 km south-west of Epping. The ramparts stand on the east side of the road, and are clearly visible from the road, though not signposted. There is a small car-parking area.

The other supposed *Ambros*— sites in Essex are at Amberden, near Debden (map ref TL 56 30); Amberland, at Roydon (TL 41 09); Amberland, Folly Lane, Walthamstow (TQ 36 91); Amberley, in Stebbing (TL 67 24); *Ambyrmede* (lost); Wickham Bishops (TL 84 13); and Emberdon, at Matching (TL 53 13).

Asheldham

Earliest known form of name: **Hain(c)tuna** 1086 (DB), then **Assild(e)ham** (twelfth century)
Derivation: the later name means 'the home of Aeschild'

The promontory fort at Asheldham was first built in the Iron Age, its defences facing east and south against the threat of seaborne assault.[52] The 6½ hectare fort survived the Roman conquest and occupation, as did a rectilinear field and road pattern imposed, probably by the Romans, on the Dengie landscape. Modern archaeological study of old maps and surviving field and parish boundaries has enabled much of this rectilinear pattern to be recovered.[53]

Asheldham fort was one of a small number of Iron Age forts known to have been re-used by Saxons as convenient defensive points (others are at Danbury and Downham). Saxon pottery has been found at the fort, as well as a knife and a throwing axe of a Danish style from the ninth century[54] suggesting that the remains of a brushwood causeway once crossed the western gateway of the fort.

Excavations at Asheldham church revealed the presence of a Saxon settlement half a kilometre from the fort – perhaps the fort was a place of refuge for such villagers during raids across the Dengie peninsula. Much of the fort's interior was destroyed by pre-war gravel extraction,[55] but the external defending embankments survive in quite good order. The field containing the fort is crossed by a public footpath, from which the fortifications can be seen; the north side is particularly impressive.

The church of St Lawrence, now redundant and used as a 'youth church', lies a short distance to the east. It has been the subject of an intensive archaeological survey[56] which showed that it was not the rather ordinary fourteenth-century church which it appeared to be. Rather it had been altered and repaired in at least nine successive phases, having started life as a timber church in the tenth or eleventh century. It was rebuilt in stone in the eleventh century, in a style which, although apparently Norman, could equally be late Anglo-Saxon.[57] In the mid-fourteenth century the nave and tower were demolished and replaced; all that survives from the Conquest-period phase is a fragment of diaper (diamond-pattern) work in the interior south wall of the nave.

Location: Asheldham lies at the centre of the Dengie peninsula's confusing road grid. Approaching from South Woodham Ferrers, take the B1012. From Maldon, take the B1018. Both these roads merge with the B1010 to Burnham-on-Crouch. At Althorne, take the B1020 to Southminster (nearest station). Asheldham lies about 2 km beyond. The road bends round to avoid the Iron Age camp. There is some parking on the north side by the public footpath and next to a waste tip entrance. Asheldham church, which is kept locked, lies half a kilometre beyond. Bradwell-on-Sea lies near enough for motorists to combine the two in a single trip.

Ashingdon
Earliest known form of name: **Assandun** 1016
Derivation: asses' hill, or *Assa*'s hill?

On St Luke's Day (18 October) 1016 a battle took place which was to change the course of English history. It was a battle which saw the end of English rule in England, which was instead to be ruled by Danish kings for a generation. Such was the Battle of Assandun, though its fame has been obscured by uncertainty over its site.

Assandun was definitely in Essex; this much we are told by the *Anglo-Saxon Chronicle*, but there are two claimants to the site. These are Ashdon on the Essex–Cambridgeshire border north-east of Saffron Walden, and Ashingdon in south-east Essex. Ashingdon was *Nesenduna* in Domesday Book, later Assendon (1198), while Ashdon was *Ascenduna* (hill covered with ash trees) in Domesday Book. Either of these place-names could have been Assandun, so the choice is usually decided by reference to the contemporary texts about the

3

battle. Ashingdon is generally preferred to Ashdon, although there would seem to be evidence to support both.

The *Anglo-Saxon Chronicle* states it thus:

The host [of Cnut's marauders] went back up into Essex, and made their way into Mercia, destroying everything before them. When the king [Edmund Ironside] learnt that the host had appeared on the scene, then for the fifth time he called up all the people of England and followed them up, overtaking them in Essex, at the hill called Ashingdon, and there a fierce battle was fought. Then ealdorman Eadric did as he had so often done before; he and the *Magesaete* [men from Herefordshire and south Shropshire] were the first to set the example of flight, and thus he betrayed his royal lord and all the people of England. Cnut was victorious and won all England by his victory. Among the slain were bishop Eadnoth, abbot Wulfsige, ealdorman Aelfric, ealdorman Godwine, Ulfcytel from East Anglia, and Aethelweard, son of ealdorman Aelfwine, and all the flower of the English nation.[58]

The battle was the climax of several years' marauding by Cnut, who was only twenty-three in 1016. Edmund was forced to seek peace, and the kingdom was divided with Cnut. However, Edmund conveniently died shortly afterwards in mysterious circumstances, and Cnut became master of all England. In 1020 he returned again to Assandun where he 'had built there a minster of stone and lime for the souls of men who were killed there; and he gave it to his own priest, whose name was Stigand.'[59]

The twelfth-century Latin work *Chronicon ex Chronicis*, by the monk 'Florence' of Worcester, gives further details: 'Cnut led his troops by slow march down to level ground . . . Edmund moved his forces rapidly and fell suddenly on the enemy.'[60] So we know hilly ground was involved as well as a church built in 1020, and we know that Cnut was heading back through Essex to his ships, probably moored somewhere along the Thames, after raiding Mercia. Hadstock church near Ashdon is certainly of the early eleventh century. Ashingdon church is no earlier than *c.* 1300,[61] though a silver coin of Cnut was found in the churchyard. Ashdon is indeed on high ground, but Ashingdon's hill, while not so high, is a marked and quite dramatic feature of that area's landscape. Ashdon is also some way inland; Edmund sallying out of London to cut off Cnut from his ships would more naturally make for the creeks and inlets of south-east

Essex than press north to meet Cnut head on. Indeed, the Chronicle states that Edmund *overtook* Cnut, implying a race for a strategic objective.

Standing on Ashingdon hilltop and looking east to Canewdon it is easy to imagine Edmund's forces charging down the hill toward's Cnut's men in the valley below, the scent of victory in English nostrils, then the treachery of Eadric's wing fleeing the battle, and the engulfing of the English by exultant Danes.

Recent topographical study appears to have strengthened Ashdon's case as it now seems possible that there was an earlier now vanished and forgotten minster church in Ashdon itself. Only archaeology will confirm that suggestion, but there is an argument not previously advanced against Hadstock church being Cnut's minster. At St Botolph's, Hadstock, built in the early eleventh century, the north door is the original door from the same date, a great rarity. This door was once covered in a so-called 'Daneskin', part of which is preserved in Saffron Walden Museum. A number of church doors claim 'Daneskin' coverings; there is a largely east-country tradition that Danish pirates captured were flayed alive and their skins nailed up on the nearest church door as an awful warning. However, virtually no church doors date back as far as the Danish raids, and where 'Daneskins' have been tested scientifically, they have nearly always been shown to be animal hide. There is only one place where a scientifically tested 'Daneskin' hanging on a pre-Norman door has been shown to be real human skin, and that is at *Hadstock*.[62] Cnut would hardly have approved of a 'Daneskin' on the door of his new minster!

The present-day Danes have little doubt at any rate that Ashingdon is the site of *Assandun* – in 1951 Prince Georg of Denmark visited the church and presented it with a model of a Viking ship and a Danish flag which can still be seen within the church. Although dating only from c. 1300, there are some puzzling features to St Andrew's, Ashingdon. Foundations discovered during grave-digging show that the church once extended further to the east. The south wall is built on very deep foundations, while the north wall has a very poor base. The south wall may mark the line of Cnut's original, narrow, church, but the north wall was moved out to widen the building. The whole church suffers from continual movement; why was it rebuilt in the first place? One suggestion[63] is that the original building was demolished after Bishop Baldock's enquiry very early in the fourteenth century into idolatry at the church. An 'idol' in the church drew large crowds daily, especially childless women, who crawled up the hill on their knees. Destruction and rebuilding may have been the only way to purge the site of these pagan assocations.

Location: Ashingdon church, which is normally kept open, lies at the end of Church Road, itself off Ashingdon Road, which runs between Rochford and the Canewdon road. Nearest station, Rochford (3 km).

Barking

Earliest known form of name: (in) **Berecingum** *c. 735*
Derivation: dwellers among the birch trees (?)

Barking Abbey was not only the earliest recorded monastic house in Essex, but also became the most important nunnery in England.[64] The abbey was founded by St Erkenwald (Bishop of London 675–93), traditionally in 666, for his sister St Ethelburga. It remained for some time a double foundation, that is, for both monks and nuns (though with separate quarters for each!). The Venerable Bede, writing *c. 735*, noted many of the miracles said to have occurred during Barking Abbey's early years, basing his information on a lost *Life of St Ethelburga*.[65] There were several miraculous cures and mysterious lights shining from heaven, as well as visions of the afterlife.[66] When Ethelburga died *c. 675*,[67] she was succeeded as abbess by Hildelith, a saintly and determined lady who extended the influence and land-holdings of the abbey.

The exact situation of this original abbey is a much vexed question. Bede gives some tantalizing clues about the location, and archaeology has pitched in too. The first scientific excavation, in 1911, revealed the outlines visible today of the twelfth-century abbey, but nothing relating to the seventh-century building.[68] This lack of evidence led some to suggest that the original site lay west of the Roding's present course,[69] or more plausibly, on a scattered site stretching from the parish church up to Cowbridge Lane off North Street.[70] These last two theories stem from place-name evidence, but archaeology has made several attempts since 1911 to find the first abbey. Excavations were carried out in 1967 and 1971, and seventh-century structures probably associated with the abbey were found to the west of the present site in 1985–6.[71] The location yet remains an enigma, but it now seems more likely that it does after all lie very close to if not beneath the twelfth-century site. The most recent excavations, west of Abbey Road, have revealed a complex of eighth-century Saxon buildings best interpreted as an industrial site associated with the abbey. The buildings contained much re-used Roman brick, probably brought by ship from London, the base of a horizontal water-mill (only the second known from this period) geared directly to the millstone, a well, and what appears to be a tenth-century glassworks, one of only two pre-Renaissance glassworks known in western Europe.

The abbey may also have served as a trading focus west of London, acting as a staging port for vessels bound for London. Barking Abbey's history during the later Anglo-Saxon period is not well known. It was traditionally held to have been burnt down by marauding Danes in 870, and, although this tale has been viewed sceptically, excavation does indicate a discontinuity.[72] Timber analysis of the industrial site shows reconstruction after 850 on the site alignment after a period of apparent abandonment. The abbey may have been reconstituted or rebuilt early in the tenth century as a purely Benedictine nunnery,[73] and its prestige grew enormously. By 1066 it was so important that William I stayed at the abbey while a more secure headquarters – the Tower of London – was being built on land that, it should be noted, had formerly belonged to the abbey. Its abbess, Alfgiva, was treated with courtesy and her abbey's land-holdings confirmed, in startling contrast to the widespread dispossession that took place elsewhere under the Conqueror.

The abbey was rebuilt again in the twelfth century, one of the largest buildings in Essex. As in Saxon days, nearly all the post-Conquest abbesses were of royal blood or noble descent; the Abbess of Barking was the senior English abbess and ranked as a peer of the realm.[74] Dissolution took place in 1539 and the abbey was demolished almost immediately; all that remains standing is the East Gate, usually known as the Curfew Tower, with a chapel on its upper floor. Plaques in the archway give brief details of the abbey's history. Nearby, St Margaret's, as the parish church, escaped destruction, but this dates from no earlier than the thirteenth century.

Though post-Saxon, the outlines of the foundations of the medieval abbey make a pleasant walk. Climb the three stone steps set against the wall of the churchyard, and you are looking right down the length of the twelfth-century church; it is hard to imagine how impressive the abbey must have looked, over 100 m long, with a central tower and two further towers at the far end. A footpath runs down the entire length of the nave (gate to the right), and further paths indicate the location of the cloister on the right-hand side. The church and its outbuildings, such as the chapter house, infirmary etc., are indicated mainly by stone outlines in the ground, though the massive south wall of the nave to your left stands in parts at over 4 m high. St Ethelburga's traditional last resting place is at the centre of the Saints' Chapel immediately beyond the three later tombs in front of you. The remains marked out form only part of the abbey buildings, which stretched west and north across the recreation ground.

All that remains of the Saxon abbey is part of an elaborately carved stone cross, which was found built into the churchyard wall in 1911[75] and dates from the tenth century.[76] The fragment, slightly tapering, is about 28 cm high, 23 x 18 cm at the base, and is one of only four items of pre-Conquest carved stonework known in Essex. It is at present displayed within St Margaret's Church, in the north-east pier of the tower. Also in the church, in the south aisle, there is an imaginative reconstruction showing how the twelfth-century abbey may have looked, and a plan of the abbey – inexplicably there is no interpretative plan on site.

In the adjacent borough of Newham stands the Passmore Edwards Museum, which houses the collections of the Essex Field Club and operates as the 'regional' museum for the five Essex-in-London boroughs and south-west Essex. Refurbished in 1990 its archaeological collections are well displayed with informative panels, photographs and diagrams to accompany them. There are a number of important Anglo-Saxon finds on display, including the latest material from Barking Abbey. This includes glass-making equipment, pins, combs and a toilet set; there is also material associated with cloth-making, including spindle-whorls, loomweights, and a pair of iron shears. From Mucking there are a number of vessels and fragments of an unusual woolcomb warmer. The Viking age is also represented. There is a sword from the River Lea, a stirrup, lance and axe from the same river, and a javelin from Walthamstow.

Location: Barking Abbey remains lie between Broadway and Abbey Road. The Curfew Tower stands opposite the end of East Street, which leads directly to Barking Station. Car parking is difficult in the area, though there are large car-parks off Abbey Road associated with the DIY superstores there. The abbey grounds are open during daylight hours. St Margaret's Church and the Curfew Tower are normally kept locked, but can be viewed by appointment (contact the rector on 081 594 2932).

The hilltop church at Ashingdon, one of the claimants for the site of the Battle of Assandun

Three tombstones mark the original location of the high altar at Barking Abbey, founded AD 666

A plaque at the parish church marks the site of the Battle of Benfleet

The mysterious pagan stone in
Beauchamp Roding churchyard

The chapel of Peter-on-the-Wall, Bradwell-on-Sea

St Nicholas Church, Castle Hedingham. The cross-shaft may be Saxon

The Saxon door of Buttsbury church

The quiet church of St Mary the Virgin, Chickney

The pre-Norman castle mound at
Clavering

The famous Saxon door of Holy
Trinity Church, Colchester

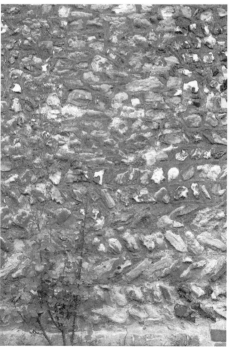

Saxon herringbone work at
Corringham church

Danbury church stands on top of an Iron Age hillfort, re-used by Saxons

The blocked Saxon window at Fobbing church

The magnificent tower of Great Tey

The striking flint church tower at
Little Bardfield

The possible remains of a stone circle at Ingatestone

The ninth-century timber staves of Greensted church – the only timber Saxon church in Britain

Passmore Edwards Museum is situated in Romford Road between Stratford and Forest Gate. The nearest BR stations are Stratford (which also has a Docklands Light Railway station) and Forest Gate. The nearest tube station is Stratford (Central Line). Parking is difficult in the area. The museum is open Wednesday to Friday, 11 a.m. to 5 p.m., Saturday, 1 p.m. to 5 p.m., and bank holidays 2 p.m. to 5 p.m. Admission is free.

Beauchamp Roding

Earliest known form of name: **Roynges Beuchamp** 1238
Derivation: one of The Rodings group of villages, meaning 'the settlement of the people of Hrotha'. Beauchamp Roding takes its name from the family of William de Beauchamp of Bedford; he owned the parish in the thirteenth century[77]

The church of St Botolph, Beauchamp Roding, stands high on a pronounced hill surrounded by fields, remote from any houses of the scattered hamlet that it serves. The church itself is of the fourteenth century, with a fifteenth-century tower. But in the churchyard, lying to the north-east of the chancel, is a monument to a far older form of worship. A large irregular stone (about 1.5 m x 1.5 m) with a slightly quartzy, sparkling, surface stands incongruously among the neat graves.

This is one of a number of such 'pagan stones' in Essex. As natural surface stone is so rare in Essex any large boulders (usually brought by glaciers during the Ice Ages and left behind when the ice retreated) would be the subject of interest to ancient man. Prominent trees, mounds and stones were often venerated and, though we know all too little about Saxon religious practices, there is every reason to assume such landmarks continued to attract devotion. In a well-known letter recorded by Bede[78] Pope Gregory instructed St Augustine on his mission to England to convert pagan shrines into Christian churches rather than destroy them.

At Beauchamp Roding a curious folk-tale about the stone survives.[79] When the church was to be built the original site selected was in the middle of the village. Because of the lack of good building stone the large hilltop stone was dragged down to the site for incorporation into the new church. Next day, however, the stone was found to have returned back up to the top of the hill. After this had happened three times, the weary villagers decided to give in to the supernatural and build the church on the hilltop. This tale seems to hint at conflict between Christianity and paganism, with Christianity eventually making a concession to paganism, precisely as directed by Pope Gregory. Until a few years ago the stone was recumbent, but it has recently been put into a standing position, which certainly enhances its air of mystery.

Beauchamp Roding is one of eight, originally nine, villages – Abbess, Aythorpe, Beauchamp, Berners, Berwick, Leaden, Margaret, White, and the now lost Morrell Roding – which straddle the upper Roding Valley. The river takes its name from the villages rather than vice versa,[80] and the river's original name is lost, although it was called the Hile, a British rather than a Saxon name, in its lower reaches. It was at one time thought that place-names originally ending in –*ingas*, of which The Rodings is one, represented the first settlements of the invading Saxons after the end of Roman rule. This view has now been shown to be false,[81] and it seems more likely that –*ingas* names represent a secondary wave of colonization. In Essex this group includes the *Berecingas* (Barking), the *Haeferingas* (Havering), and the *Eppingas/Uppingas* (Epping). All these areas lie astride Roman roads and contain a variety of land types, including a river valley.[82] It seems likely that The Rodings, and these other discrete blocks of land, formed some sort of tribal statelets before the formation of the kingdom of Essex.[83] The problem of how the East Saxon kingdom was created is discussed more fully in the introduction. Even after the kingdom was set up The Rodings formed a distinct district, which has survived, in its place-name at least, to the present day.

Location: Beauchamp Roding church lies north of Fyfield off the B184, which runs from Chipping Ongar to Leaden Roding. Opposite a minor road signposted to Woodends there is a track (suitable for cars) leading to a large parking area at the foot of the hill on which the church stands. The church is normally kept open.

Boreham
Earliest known form of name: **Borham** *c.* 1045
Derivation: unknown, perhaps 'boar enclosure'

This is a puzzling church architecturally. Most authorities[84] make the church Norman, but there has been a persistent belief that parts of it are Saxon. In particular, the style of building of the chancel arch and the great central three-stage tower, in the lower part at least, has been seen as characteristically Saxon.[85] The tower has rubble walls interspersed with Roman brick, with very long narrow windows on the north and south sides. There are Saxon parallels to this elsewhere in the country, but it has to be said that certain features of Saxon and Norman building techniques are very similar; a number of 'Norman' churches have recently been shown to be Saxon, however, and others no doubt await re-interpretation.

The church is dedicated to St Andrew. There are thirty such ancient dedications in Essex, and it has been suggested that at least some of these relate to St Cedd's seventh-century mission to the East Saxons.[86] St Andrew eventually became the patron saint of Scotland, and this fisher-apostle's cult was strong in the early Celtic Church based on Iona and Lindisfarne. Cedd was a monk of Lindisfarne. This interesting theory is of course virtually impossible to prove.

Work on the church interior in 1979 did finally confirm the Saxon origin of the church.[87] The removal of plaster from the north wall of the tower exposed a Norman aumbry (a recess reserved for the communion host) cut into half the thickness of the wall; the wall at the back of this cupboard-like recess is the original Saxon chancel wall which was thickened by the Normans when they raised the height of the tower.

Location: Boreham lies on the Roman road from London to Colchester, now the B1137 since the building of the A12 bypass. The church is situated in Church Road. Turn off the B1137 (main road) on the south side at Plantation Road and this runs into Church Road. The church is normally kept locked; for access contact the vicar on 0245 467281.

Bradwell-on-Sea
Earliest known form of name: **Ythancaestir** *c.* 735 (Bede)
Derivation: the Roman fort of *Othona*

Bradwell-on-Sea lies at the far end of the Dengie peninsula.[88] Here are two stark contrasts: facing the Blackwater Estuary is Bradwell nuclear power station, producing energy at the very limits of man's technology and ingenuity, while facing the saltings, the North Sea and the east wind is the chapel of St Peter-on-the-Wall, a humble stone structure built by pious hands over thirteen centuries ago.

The story of St Peter-on-the-Wall begins even further back in time. Roman Britain came under pressure from Saxon pirates in the second half of the third century, so a line of forts, known as Saxon Shore forts, were built along the south and east coast. One such fort was placed here at the strategic Blackwater Estuary. Of conventional bastioned playing-card design, the fort (and accompanying settlement) was called *Othona*. It appears to have been continuously garrisoned by the *Fortenses*, an auxiliary cavalry unit originally raised in North Africa, until Britain was stripped of troops in a forlorn effort by the British-proclaimed Emperor Constans III to usurp the western Empire. The town and port continued, however, and the place-name survived the arrival of the East Saxons. It was known to Bede as *Ythancaestir*, the suffix *caestir* (pronounced 'chester') being the Old English form of the Late Latin *castra*, and invariably used to describe abandoned Roman fortifications wherever they found them.[89] This isolated Roman fort, by then ruinous, was destined to play a singular role in the history of Essex.

Everything that we know about the role of *Ythancaestir* in the conversion of Essex to Christianity is derived from the writings of Bede. When the Romans relinquished control of Britain, the island relapsed into paganism except for the westernmost parts. The Saxons brought their own religion with them when they arrived. One far-flung Christian outpost which did flourish was in Scotland, at Iona, founded from Ireland by St Columba in 563. In 635 a monk from Iona, Aidan, crossed the country to found a new monastery at Lindisfarne. Aidan was anxious to evangelize the heathen Anglo-Saxons, and trained twelve young Englishmen to begin the task.

One of these was Cedd who, after considerable success in the Midlands, came to Essex at the appeal of King Sigeberht *Sanctus* in 653. Sigeberht *Sanctus* had already been converted at the court of his friend, King Oswiu of Northumbria, and was now anxious for the conversion of his people.

Cedd, with an unnamed companion, travelled among the people of Essex 'and established a strong Christian community', as Bede reports.[90] Cedd went back to Northumbria to receive the title of Bishop of the East Saxons, then returned to continue his work. As Bede says,

> He built churches in several places and ordained priests and deacons to assist in teaching the Faith and baptizing the people, especially in the city which the Saxons call *Ythancaestir* and that called *Tilaburg*.[91]

We do not know where Cedd's other East Saxon churches were founded, apart from those at Bradwell-on-Sea and East Tilbury (see separate entry). Traditional Ceddan foundations include Prittlewell and West Mersea (see separate entries). St Peter-on-the-Wall at Bradwell-on-Sea was, however, the principal foundation of this apostle of Essex.

In 664 Cedd was called to the momentous Synod of Whitby, which ended the differences between the Roman and Celtic Churches. Cedd acted as interpreter between the different parties at the synod, and the Roman interest prevailed, thus closing that brief chapter of Essex history when Anglo–Celtic rites held sway. Shortly afterwards Cedd died of the plague at Lastingham monastery, one of his foundations in Yorkshire. According to Bede, thirty from his community at *Ythancaestir* went to Lastingham to honour his name, and all but one shared his fate.

The subsequent history of St Peter-on-the-Wall is not well known, but we can assume that the church suffered at the hands of the Danes, though the town seems to have survived that bloody era until the disastrous tide of 1099, which destroyed *Effecestra*, as it was recorded in Domesday Book. The population seems to have moved inland to Bradwell-on-Sea (which is in fact some distance from the coast!), though the church remained a chapel-of-ease at least until the Reformation. By the seventeenth century it had been converted into a barn and its long history forgotten until the beginning of this century, when it was restored, and finally re-consecrated in 1920.

This chapel of St Peter-on-the-Wall then was built some time between 653 and 664; it is one of a very few surviving seventh-century churches, and a unique and precious treasure for Essex. It was built from materials salvaged from the ruins of the Roman fort, straddling the wall of the fort (hence the name) where the Roman road entered the western gateway. Its foundations still rest on the old Roman road. The chapel was originally built with an apse at the eastern end, two small side-chambers, and a porch at the western end. These have now disappeared, though their foundations are marked out in concrete. The surviving nave is about 16 m long by about 7 m wide.

Little is left of the Roman fort of *Othona*. Much of the wall, stretching out to the saltings, was still exposed in 1864 when extensive excavations recovered many domestic objects but no building plans. Today, however, all that is left of these 4 m thick walls is a very small section to the south on the edge of the rough ground by the cottage.

Inside the chapel a striking modern altar was dedicated in 1985, supported by three stone pillars, one from Lindisfarne, one from Iona, and one from Lastingham. A fitting tribute to Cedd and those pioneers of Christian mission.

Location: Bradwell-on-Sea is at the end of the B1021 from Burnham-on-Crouch. This road is joined by the B1020 at Southminster (nearest railway station), which runs eventually to South Woodham Ferrers as the B1012, and Maldon as the B1010. The Dengie peninsula's road network is very intricate and it is very easy to take a wrong turning! At Bradwell-on-Sea village turn off at the parish church onto Eastend Road, signposted to St Peter's. This is in fact the old Roman road to *Othona*. The road ends in a car-park about 1 km before the chapel, and the rest of the journey is on foot. The chapel is always kept open, and souvenirs and an excellent guidebook are normally available.

Broomfield

Earliest known form of name: **Brumfeldam** 1086 (DB)
Deviation: broom-covered open country

Broomfield church has one of only six ancient round towers in Essex, and its handsome outline topped by a shingled spire makes a pleasant backdrop to Church Green, itself a haven from the roar of the traffic on the main road.

There is much Roman brick in the fabric of the tower, which is otherwise mainly of mortared flint. Flint is a very difficult material to build with as its sheer weight means that it requires battens while the mortar sets. The grace of the tower is therefore a tribute to the Norman builders, who worked with the only local stone which was plentifully available. In the south wall of the nave and near the door,[92] however, is a different type of stone – a huge piece of chocolate-brown pudding-stone actually projecting from the nave wall, almost like a little step to nowhere. This pudding-stone – a conglomerate rock composed of rounded pebbles – may once have been free-standing, or at least a large object of awe in a field. As at Beauchamp Roding, it may have been felt advisable by the church authorities to demonstrate the power of the church over such superstition. But while Beauchamp Roding's 'pagan stone' was left in the churchyard, at Broomfield the stone was incorporated into the fabric of the building in such a way as to make it very obvious that it had been so incorporated. So there the stone sits today, half in and half out. There are a number of churches in Essex where the fabric has been erected actually over these prominent pudding-stones to show the church triumphant indeed, but none are quite so odd as Broomfield's. There seems to be no other explanation than that of ancient worship, by pagan Saxons, and older peoples still, sublimated and subsumed by the Christian church.

Down Broomfield's main road to Chelmsford, near the post office, stands an insignificant road called Clobb's Yard. While digging for gravel behind Clobb's Yard in 1888 and 1894 a remarkable and unique assemblage of early Saxon material was recovered. Here a great noble, perhaps from the East Saxon royal family, had been laid to rest in the seventh century. His chamber grave had probably been robbed previously, and then partly destroyed by the gravel-digging, but even so what was found was enough to cast some light on how a great lord might live in the Kingdom of Essex.

The finest objects were of gold: a tiny but exquisite golden pyramid set with garnets that originally formed part of a sword fitting; a gold tongue-plate also inlaid with garnets and blue glass, from a strap or belt; and a strip of gold filigree from a belt buckle. Also found were a wooden bucket, two cherry-wood cups with gilt copper rims, a Frankish-style pot, two blue glass jars, an iron lamp on a tripod, an iron sword in a wooden scabbard, and a bronze bowl containing a cow's horn. Stylistically, the burial goods have parallels with other rich and contemporary burials at Taplow (now in Buckinghamshire, but then just beyond the western frontier of Essex)[93] and at Sutton Hoo, the royal burial ground of the East Anglians.[94]

These finds are now preserved in the British Museum, and nothing remains of or commemorates the barrow at Broomfield. A watching brief undertaken by an Essex County Council archaeologist in 1985 found no further grave goods, though there was some domestic pottery hinting at an otherwise unknown settlement site in the vicinity.[95]

If the visitor makes the short trip into Chelmsford, the Cathedral is worth a visit. In the south transept are two mid-nineteenth-century windows portraying the East Saxon saints St Osyth and St Ethelburga. It is interesting in passing to note the differences in the way such characters are represented over the ages since they lived; for instance, the fifteenth-century statue of King Saberht in Westminster Abbey (see entry under Sites in Other Counties, City of London) is very much in the spirit of its age, portraying him as a Renaissance prince. Near the Cathedral at County Hall, the Council Chamber and ante-room are decorated with imaginative scenes from the history of

Essex (John Ball at Brentwood in 1381, Queen Elizabeth at Tilbury in 1588, etc.), together with two huge maps of Essex, one as it was in medieval times, one modern, and coats-of-arms of all the Essex boroughs. Around the chamber is a frieze of names of the Saxon kings of Essex and the supposed dates of their rule. The names and dates are given as follows:

> ERCHWINE *c.* 527, SLEDDA 587, ST SEBERT 597, SAXRED 614, SIGEBERT I 617, SIGEBERT II 623, SIGEBERT III 655, SIGERIC & SEBBA 663, SIGENARD 693, OFFA 700, SELRED 709, SWITHRED 738, SIGERIC 792, SIGERED 799

At the Chelmsford and Essex Museum three galleries have been given over to a new display, 'The Story of Chelmsford'. This has a small section on the Saxon period, which includes a display panel about the early pagan cemetery at Springfield Lyons, a case of small domestic items from various Chelmer Valley locations, and a part of one of the cherry-wood cups with gilt copper rims from the Broomfield burial on loan from the British Museum. There is also a map showing Saxon/Medieval settlement sites in the Chelmer Valley.

Location: Broomfield church lies about 3½ km from Chelmsford town centre along the old A130 (now B1008). Follow signs for Broomfield Hospital. The nearest station is at Chelmsford. The church stands beside Church Green and there is a small parking area. The church is normally kept locked but the pudding-stone is visible from the exterior. County Hall is in Duke Street, as is the Cathedral (hidden away down Church Lane). Visits to the County Hall Council Chamber can be arranged through the County Public Relations and Information Office on 0245–492211. There is also an annual open day (date variable). The Chelmsford and Essex Museum stands in Oaklands Park, Moulsham Street, at the A414 roundabout. It is open Monday to Saturday, 10 a.m. to 5 p.m. and Sunday, 2 p.m. to 5 p.m. Admission is free.

Buttsbury
Earliest known form of name: **Botolfvespirie** 1219
Derivation: Botolph's pear tree

As noted by Reaney,[96] there is still a Perry Street south of Little Blunts Farm, a road which must also have taken its name from the same pear tree.

The tiny church of St Mary, with its brick tower and wooden belfry, is isolated in fields looking down over the Wid, about as remote as anywhere can be in populous mid-Essex. There are fine views across towards Ingatestone, and several church spires visible up and down the gentle valley – a typical Essex scene. Here at this church is a great and rare treasure, though in a poor state of preservation. The north door (on the opposite side to the main porch) is made from wood hewn before the Conqueror ever set foot in England. There are only two pre-Conquest doors in the whole country, and both of them are in Essex. This is one of them, and the other is at Hadstock.[97] The door, which is not in its original position, has a little grille set into its timbers, and some fine ornamental ironwork from the thirteenth century, the terminals of which seem almost zoomorphic (suggestive of animal-shapes). When we visited the church it was being re-roofed and having the rendering stripped off, revealing pudding-stones and much Roman brick. Some of the masonry was set in an interesting herring-bone fashion, suggestive of Saxon workmanship, though the nave is usually assigned to the fourteenth century.

Before Botolph's pear tree was even a pip, Buttsbury's original name was *Cingam*, first recorded in Domesday Book[98] and one of a group of parishes south-west of Chelmsford with this name. The others are Fryerning (*Inga* in 1086, *Ginges* in 1291), Ingatestone (*Inga* in 1086, *Ginges* in 1241), Ingrave (*Inga* in 1086, *Ginge* in 1248), Margaretting (*Ginga* in 1086), and Mountnessing (*Ginga* in 1086). Also, in East Horndon is the farm of Fouchers, but known at the time of Domesday as *Ginga*. As Reaney summarizes so concisely,[99] 'this extensive district must once have had a single name, which . . . was *Gigingas* or *Gegingas*'.

This name seems to mean 'the dwellers in the district'. Place-names including the element –ge– are generally thought to denote the very earliest phase of Saxon settlement: other examples in Essex are Vange (the fen district) and Dengie (the district of the Daenningas). As noted under the entries for Asheldham and Corringham, these districts, also known by the Latin title of *regiones*, comprise discrete blocks of land seized by or handed over to the first Saxon settlers intact. Usually there is a mix of land-types providing a mix of resources in the district, and *Ginge* is no exception. The area enclosed by the parishes above includes fertile river valleys as well as higher ground, and it also straddles the strategic Roman road to Colchester, giving control over trade. This is another characteristic of these early settlements.[100]

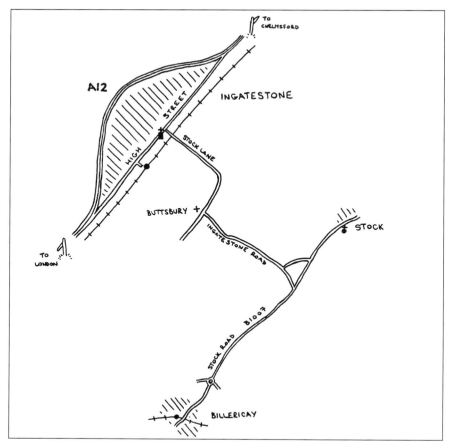

Buttsbury church

Location: Buttsbury is now so small a hamlet that its very name has disappeared from the Ordnance Survey 1:50,000 sheets, which is no doubt as great a source of resentment to local inhabitants as it is an irritant to visitors. The parish lies directly between Billericay and Ingatestone. If approaching from Ingatestone (nearest station), turn into Stock Lane by the parish church and follow the road, which bends sharply once it has crossed the Wid, for about 2 km. The church lies at the junction with a lane leading south. If approaching from Billericay follow the B1007 towards Stock. About 1 km before Stock there is a lane signposted to Ingatestone. Follow this for about 2.5 km, when the aforementioned junction is reached. The church, which is kept locked, is on an awkward bend and screened behind trees. Parking is difficult, though vehicles could draw up on the grassy area to the south of the church where a track crosses the fields to Ingatestone.

18

Canewdon: see entry for Great Stambridge

Castle Hedingham
Earliest known form of name: **Haingheham** 1086 (DB)
Derivation: The *ham* of the people of Headda, or *ham* of the dwellers by the hythe (meaning 'harbour')

The history of this village has been dominated by Hedingham Castle since Aubrey de Vere first built it in the twelfth century. The story of the de Veres, one of England's greatest families for centuries, is a fascinating one. Those interested can follow the story of their fortunes by a visit to the castle, which contains excellent and informative displays about its own history and the function of castles generally. It is undoubtedly one of the finest and most complete twelfth-century castles in all England.

However, it is to the village we turn, in search of the work of Saxon hands. The village itself has great charm; there is an abundance of fine architecture, timbered, Georgian and later. Tea-shops and inns are welcoming, the shops interesting, and there is a general air of being used to the comings and goings of visitors. A typical church in Essex was built by many hands in several styles over many generations, and St Nicholas at Castle Hedingham is no exception. It is a veritable palimpsest of styles; essentially Norman fabric, a Tudor brick tower, an ornate fifteenth-century rood-screen and a remarkable sixteenth-century double hammerbeam roof. There were also extensive renovations in the last century, which unfortunately resulted in the disposal of what was believed to have been the Saxon font. Replaced by a Victorian font, it was said to have been buried near the south door.[101]

Inside the church, there is a curious carved stone on the south wall of the south aisle, known traditionally as the Saxon Stone. It is a crudely carved though evocative stone with the face and trunk of a penitential figure, hands joined in prayer. It is not clear who is supposed to be represented; a priest or St Mary Magdalene have been suggested. Its date is unknown, and it could be Saxon, though from stylistic evidence it is more usually ascribed to the Norman period.

St Nicholas is fortunate to possess three Norman doors in three Norman doorways. One of them, the south door, is one of a clutch of Essex church doors claiming to have once been covered by a 'Daneskin'. The skin that was nailed to this door is not necessarily claimed to have been an actual Dane's skin, however, simply that of a thief who tried to rob the church. Other 'Daneskin' doors are known at Copford and East Thurrock, but the only one to be plausibly pre-Norman and human is that at Hadstock (see separate entry).

Outside the church, in the churchyard, is a most equivocal monument. Now in the form of a war memorial, and surmounted by a cross, the square-section central column once stood in the cellar of the Falcon, an old coaching inn in nearby Falcon Square. There it supported the main beam of the ceiling until 1921, when it was re-erected in the churchyard to serve with more fitting prominence. The shaft possibly formed part of a cross originally; the village green at Castle Hedingham is still known as Crouch Green, from Anglo-Saxon *cruc*, meaning 'cross'. One theory is that the cross was thrown down at the time of the Reformation, only to be re-used by the canny host of the Falcon.[102] Attempts to date the shaft are based on its decoration. There is an elaborate floral pattern running up all four sides in a Norman style, but on the hollowed angles of the edges there are carved bosses very much in the Saxon style. Was it a Saxon cross re-cut later by Normans? Or was it commissioned by Normans and made locally by one still familiar with the old Saxon styles? We are never likely to know the answer, but as one writer puts it, 'the important thing for the present-day viewer is that together with the ancient stonework and carvings, the cross in its present form is of singular beauty'.[103]

Location: Castle Hedingham is on the B1058 road to Sudbury (nearest station – 8 km). The B1058 runs off the main A604 5 km north of Halstead. The church of St Nicholas is normally kept open.

Chelmsford: see entry for Broomfield

Chickney

Earliest known form of name: **Cicchenai** 1086 (DB)
Derivation: Cicca's island is perhaps the best interpretation of this name; the parish is almost surrounded by three streams

Chickney is one of the smallest parishes in Essex. Its little church stands at the end of a long tree-arched lane and, though now redundant, it is normally kept open. This is fortunate, as it is a fine if little-known Saxon church. Dedicated to St Mary the Virgin, it is a gem of virtually unaltered Saxon architecture; the rough nave and the chancel as far as the sanctuary are all pre-Conquest work. The rest of the chancel dates from the thirteenth century, while the tower was added in the fourteenth century and the porch in the fifteenth. Because it entirely escaped Norman alteration, and consists only of Saxon and Early English styles, it has been well described as an 'essentially English' church.[104] As noted in the excellent guide produced by the Redundant Churches Fund,[105] and as visitors can see for themselves, the nave is definitely not quite square in plan. Also, the tower and chancel were not built square onto the nave, so the whole effect is one of odd angles in the interior. There are Saxon splayed windows in the nave and chancel, those in the nave are doubly splayed (though the one on the north side is partly obscured) – with only these tiny windows for light, it must have been very dark inside the original Saxon building. The fabric itself is flint and pebble rubble, partly plaster-covered. Chickney church's isolated position probably saved it from architectural alteration down the ages, so that a visit today will give a vivid impression of what a remote church in Saxon Essex looked like.

Location: Chickney lies between Stansted Mountfitchet and Thaxted off the B1051. It is most scenically approached on foot by the path running north-east from the B1051. The church is normally kept open.

Clavering
Earliest known form of name: **Claefring** 1050
Derivation: place where clover grows

In 1051 Edward the Confessor had been on the throne for nine years. Edward's reign has been characterized as one of weak monarchy and a strong nobility,[106] and in 1051 the greatest of the nobles was Godwine, Earl of Wessex, whose earldom stretched from Land's End to Thanet. However, a rival power-base was emerging; that of the parvenu Norman lords and their officials who had begun settling across England at the king's invitation. This rivalry came to a head in 1051 when there was a riot at Dover between the townspeople and the retinue of Count Eustace of Boulogne, a prominent Norman, over the billeting of the count's men. About twenty were killed, on either side. The count complained to the king, who ordered Godwine to harry the town, the usual method of Anglo-Saxon collective punishment. But Dover lay within Godwine's own earldom, and he refused to obey the orders.

Godwine had decided upon a showdown with his rivals, and he and his sons assembled an army which marched on the king at Gloucester, in an attempt to force the king's hand. But Godwine's men would not wage war against the king and he had to back down. Edward sent the family into exile, and the Norman faction grew stronger at court. But by September 1052 Godwine had returned to England with a strong force, and this time the king was forced to concede. After besieging London, Godwine and his family were restored to all their previous lands and titles, and the Normans were ousted.

This is where Essex, and Clavering, come on the scene. The *Anglo-Saxon Chronicle* records the Norman downfall:

> When Archbishop Robert and the Frenchmen found that out, they took their horses and went, some went to Osbern Pentecost's castle [in Herefordshire], some north to Robert's castle. Archbishop Robert, Bishop Ulf and their companions went out of the East Gate of London and killed or else wounded many young men. They went right on to the Naze; Robert there went out in an unseaworthy ship, fared straight over the sea and gave up his *pallium* and all Christendom in this land – just as God willed it for he had obtained that honour against God's will.[107]

The Archbishop Robert was a Norman, Robert of Jumieges, who had been translated to Canterbury from the bishopric of London only eighteen months earlier in March 1051. Bishop Ulf was another Norman, who had been appointed to the see of Dorchester-on-Thames in 1049. Their ignominious flight must have crossed Essex, following the old Roman road to Colchester. The lands of Robert and Ulf were divided up between Godwine's family.

The rest of the 'Frencysce' as the *Anglo-Saxon Chronicle* called them, fled to Osbern's castle in Herefordshire or to 'Robert's castle'. This was convincingly identified by J.H. Round[108] as Clavering Castle. 'Robert', who owned the castle, was Robert Fitzwimarc, sheriff of Essex in Edward the Confessor's time, and a noble of Breton descent. His family remained important after the Conquest; his son Swein held Clavering Hundred (among other places) at the time of Domesday Book.

The ultimate fate of these besieged Normans is unknown, though most Normans were declared outlaws shortly after their fall from grace. The king had been humiliated by Godwine's show of strength, and Godwine's ascendancy was undisputed. Ironically, he did not live long enough to enjoy the fruits of his scheming – he died the following year. However, his earldom went to his son Harold, who ultimately went on to reach for the crown itself in the fateful year of 1066.

A visit to Clavering today will be rewarded with a fine prospect of the motte of Clavering Castle, one of twenty-six castles in Essex with some visible remains. Situated adjacent to Clavering parish church, the squarish mound covers an impressive area. More remarkable still is the fact that this castle was built of stone rather than timber, perhaps the earliest in the county to be so constructed.[109] This technique of building stone castles was, of course, a Norman import, carried out in the last days of Anglo-Saxon rule. The moat (*mainly dry*) is still of formidable width and depth. The mound on which the castle stood is roughly rectangular, about 100 m long and 50 m broad. The castle sits in a bend of the Stort. Though it is only a stream today, ramparts in the hollow of the river bend indicate that it was once powerful enough to drive a mill, as the pattern of the earthworks is characteristic of a dam and reservoir.[110] The castle mound itself is heavily overrun with trees and a dense mat of undergrowth – a winter visit will give a better idea of the site's scale. Nothing, however, is left of the masonry that must have caused such astonishment when it was first put up.

Location: Clavering lies on the B1038 from Newport (nearest station). The site is best approached from the church, which lies down a narrow lane off the main street. The castle lies to the north of the churchyard; a footpath from the churchyard leads straight to the remains. Parking is difficult in the immediate area.

Coggeshall: see entry for White Notley

Colchester
Earliest known form of name: **Colneceastre** *c*. 925 (ASC)
Derivation: the (Roman) fortress of *Colonia*

Colchester's proudest boast is that it is Britain's oldest recorded town, a fact which has earned it inclusion in the *Guinness Book of Records*. Today, Colchester's Roman, medieval and Civil War remains make the town an important tourist centre. Before the Roman Conquest, Colchester, *Camulodunum*, was the 'capital' of Cunobelin's kingdom.

Cunobelin – Shakespeare's Cymbeline – held sway over much of southern Britain before the Roman invasion of AD 43, and *Camulodunum* included military, religious, industrial and domestic sites in an area stretching from the Colne to the Roman River, but particularly at Sheepen and Gosbecks. The Roman city, established as *Colonia Claudia Victricensis*, remained important throughout the Roman period, though in common with many other urban centres it suffered decline during the later Empire.

The mechanism by which Colchester was transferred from Roman to Saxon hands is not clear, but during excavations at Lion Walk in the 1970s the remains of two Saxon sunken huts were found. One hut, simple in design, was dated to the fifth century while the second was later – sixth- or seventh-century – and had been built against the wall of a Roman house. This implies dereliction and abandonment.[111] A further group of Saxon huts was found at the Culver Street site in the 1980s, and Saxon pottery has been found in all parts of the town, as well as Saxon pits at North Hill in 1965. It has been suggested that this early Saxon settlement derived from Germanic mercenaries deliberately stationed in the town to defend it.[112]

In the later Saxon period Colchester's history is obscure, and it may have been virtually deserted. However, its strong walls still stood, and attracted the attention of Danes in the tenth century. The East Anglian Danes seem to have occupied Colchester early in that century and its fortifications must have made it a substantial 'forward base' near the English frontier. Edward the Elder was, however, doggedly pursuing a policy of reconquest, establishing *burhs* (forts, fortified strongholds) as strong points, moving the frontier forward, and establishing further *burhs*. By the autumn of 917, after a prolonged campaign in the south Midlands against the Danes, Edward's men were ready to move on Colchester. The *Anglo-Saxon Chronicle* notes,

A great force gathered together in the autumn, from Kent, Surrey, and Essex, and from all parts from the nearest fortresses, and marched on Colchester and surrounded the fortress and attacked until they had captured it: they slew all the inhabitants, and seized everything inside, except the men who escaped over the wall.[113]

A Danish counter-attack against Maldon was beaten off, and Edward 'went with the West Saxon levies to Colchester, and repaired and rebuilt it where it had been destroyed'.[114] The submission of all the East Anglian Danes followed.

24

The Roman town walls which failed to keep out Edward the Elder's men still encircle the town and a full circuit makes a pleasant walk. The Balkerne Gate on the west side, one of the best surviving Roman gates in Britain, was blocked during the late Saxon period, and this blocking-up is usually ascribed to Edward the Elder's refortification in 917.[115]

Colchester was in fact systematically redeveloped after the re-conquest; new streets were laid out and new properties established along the High Street and extending southwards to Culver Street. Further subdivisions of the town were created, based on multiples of the pole – an old lineal measurement. This radical departure from the Roman street plan implies strong central, and therefore royal, authority for the improvements.[116]

Turning to the castle itself, it has of course been known for some time that this great work, the largest Norman keep in the country, is built on the podium of the Roman temple. At the end of the Roman period the temple underwent alterations, implying that it first lost its religious status and became an audience hall, then perhaps a defensible residence or place of refuge as there was no longer sufficient manpower to guard the whole town wall circuit.[117]

Links between this sub-Roman use and the tenth-century re-founding are elusive, but it now seems that the re-founding saw the conversion of the temple site, and whatever ruins lay on it, into a *villa regalis*, a royal administrative centre.[118] This *villa regalis* included a chapel, which probably lay adjacent to the later Norman bailey chapel, the foundations of which are on view on the south side of the castle. The Saxon chapel would have been a wooden one, and it apparently possessed elaborate wall-paintings, remains of which have been discovered.[119] To the south of this and on a similar alignment stood a hall building which may have been the centre from which the estate was managed – the function, if any, of the temple ruins is unknown. This building stood (very approximately) where the Castle public house now stands, but no sign of it remains.

To the south, St Nicholas and All Saints Churches, standing at either end of the Roman basilica, may also have originated in the tenth century.[120] All Saints Church still stands, now a museum of natural history, and St Nicholas is commemorated in St Nicholas Street. The remains of the Saxon church of St John's were discovered in the 1970s during works for the new St Botolph's roundabout, though no remains are preserved for public view. On the north-west corner of the castle precinct, St Helen's Chapel stands on the site of the town's Roman theatre, and indeed incorporates some of its standing walls. This too may have been founded in the tenth century,[121] though an earlier date in the reign of Offa (757–94) has also been suggested.[122]

The question of continuity remains tantalizing. A 'minimum area of continuous occupation' in or around the castle precinct has been postulated,[123] with other foci of settlement outside the walls. Literary and folklore sources can assist archaeology in investigating Colchester's 'Dark Age'. The presence of a holy well dedicated to St Anne in Colchester indicates the continuance and christianization of pagan well-worship which would be virtually impossible to prove archaeologically.

Colchester has long been associated with an eponymous 'Coel' ('Old King Cole') and with St Helena, the mother of Constantine the Great and discoverer of the True Cross, which still forms the arms of Colchester. The Balkerne Gate was originally known as Colkyngs Castle, the castle itself was 'King Cole's Palace', and there was a 'King Coyle's Pump' in the High Street. Much of the legendary material about Coel and Helena derives from Geoffrey of Monmouth's *History of the Kings of Britain*. The fact that this is a largely fictitious work has not prevented a number of theories being erected on its superstructure, and the matter is confused by a real 'King Cole', known as *Coel Hen*, who seems to have been a sub-Roman ruler in the English north country and Scottish Lowlands.[124]

There is, however, a *local* Colchester tradition which *pre-dates* Geoffrey of Monmouth's work.[125] This is recorded in the early twelfth-century *Colchester Chronicle*, an annal which was later incorporated into the *Red Parchment* or *Oath Book of Colchester*, a fourteenth-century compilation, and it also occurs separately in the Bodleian MS Gough 1, a manuscript of ecclesiastical origin and relating to St John's Abbey, Colchester, though in the form of a late copy from the sixteenth century only. The chronicle is the only nearly contemporary source for the Norman origins of the castle, and contains information not recorded elsewhere, such as the claim that Eudo Dapifer, the builder of Colchester Castle, restored St Helen's Chapel and gave it to St John's. There is also material relating to Coel and Helena, legendary but different to the Geoffrey of Monmouth material and so from a different source.

It has been suggested that this chronicle was complied at St John's, originally in the form of a grand 'history' of the town from its legendary foundation by 'Coel'.[126] It seems likely that the great antiquity of the fabric of St Helen's Chapel was recognized, and this may have given rise to the chronicle legend that it was built by Helena's own hands,[127] in an attempt by the chroniclers to link the chapel's dedication to the Roman phase of the town's history. Similarly with the castle. Its Roman origin and sub-Roman re-use may have been recognized, and even some memory of this preserved, in the *Colchester Chronicle*'s claim that the Norman keep was constructed *in fundo palacii Coelis quondam regis* – on the foundation of the palace of Coel, formerly king.[128]

Today, Colchester Castle houses the best display in the county of antiquities relating to Essex history. Under the collective title of 'Our English Heritage', three cases on the first floor cover the Anglo-Saxon period. The first, 'Anglo-Saxon Settlement *c.* 450–650', contains a variety of domestic and funerary artefacts as well as plans and diagrams showing a reconstruction of one of the Lion Walk huts. In the case is sixth-century grave material from Feering, two antler combs (one from Culver Street, Colchester, one from St Osyth), and other bone and metal items from Bradwell and Little Oakley. There are two sets of grave finds from the Riverside Estate on the north-east corner of Colchester's walls, including brooches, rings and beads. There are also glass, amber and ceramic beads from the Acton Collection.

The 'Saxon and Viking Weapons' case contains a number of spearheads. Of Saxon origin and dating from the fifth to seventh centuries are two spearheads from Mersea Road, Colchester, and one from elsewhere in Colchester, as well as three seaxes; two of these date from the eighth century and were recovered from the Colne at Colchester. Also from the Colne is a fearsome Viking-type axe-head dating from the ninth to tenth centuries and an equally formidable sword of the eighth century from the Colne. Smaller finds include two shield bosses and three spear ferrules.

The case 'Late Saxons and Normans' contains various cooking pots or fragments, and the piece of 'Daneskin' found under a door hinge at Copford Church. Unlike the 'Daneskin' at Hadstock (see separate entry), the Copford skin seems too late to be Danish but the accompanying text speculates that it may have been 'someone executed for sacrilege, placed in this position as a permanent reminder of the punishment due for this crime'.

Perhaps the most familiar Anglo-Saxon monument in Colchester is Holy Trinity Church. Standing in Trinity Street, the typically Saxon triangular head of the west door is a well-known and charming Essex treasure. Only the west tower of Holy Trinity, now a museum of social history, dates from Anglo-Saxon times, being of the tenth or eleventh century. The tower is built from re-used Roman brick, and two sets of Saxon belfry windows survive. The lower windows are enlivened with a brick coursing in an arcade pattern. The tower can also be viewed from the inside, where there is a Saxon arch constructed out of Roman brick.

Location: Colchester stands on the A12 and A604 and is the hub of many lesser north Essex roads. The town has two railway stations, Colchester North, standing on the main line from Liverpool Street to East Anglia, and Colchester St Botolph, serving Clacton and Walton. Virtually the entire circuit of the Roman walls still exists and almost all of what remains can be viewed. Allow about an hour for a complete circuit. Balkerne Gate on the west side above Balkerne Hill is the most striking relic.

The Castle Museum is open from Monday to Friday, 10 a.m. to 5 p.m., Saturday 10 a.m. to 4 p.m., and from April to September on Sunday, 2.30 p.m. to 5 p.m. There is an admission charge. All Saints Church in the High Street (now a museum of natural history) is open Monday to Saturday, 10 a.m. to 1 p.m. and 2 p.m. to 5 p.m., or 2 p.m. to 4 p.m. during October to March. It is closed on Good Friday and from 24 to 26 December. Admission is free. Holy Trinity Church in Trinity Street is now a museum of social history, and has the same opening hours as All Saints Church. St Helen's Chapel in Maidenburgh Street is not open to the public, but remains of the Roman theatre, of which the chapel forms part, and an interpretative display can be seen further along Maidenburgh Street.

Corringham
Earliest known form of name: **Currincham** 1086 (DB)
Derivation: settlement of Curra's people

The glory of Corringham parish church is its massive Norman tower. The upper two stages of this belfry are arcaded and topped by 'a roof like a hat too big for it'.[129] The whole church has a very heavy and solid appearance. It is framed by some lovely chestnut trees, some of them of great age, and stands opposite a group of fine medieval buildings; the lively Bull public house is of the fifteenth century and heavily timbered, while next door is the weatherboarded Hall Farm Cottage.

This impressive example of early Norman work is, however, built on a late Saxon base. In the south walls of the chancel and nave the Saxon hand can be seen in courses of rough herringbone-pattern stone quite distinctive from the later Norman work above it. It is particularly noticeable in the lower part of the chancel wall. These parts of the wall are also not as thick as the later massive Norman work – this thinness of wall is a characteristic of Saxon building. There are also fragments of Saxon work inside the church, in the chancel arch, the north wall of the chancel, and the east wall of the tower.

Corringham is one of a trio of places, the other two being Stanford-le-Hope and Fobbing (see separate entry), at the eastern end of *The Land that Fanns* (to quote the title of Leslie Thompson's book), the Thurrock peninsula. These villages are all built on the gravel terraces overlooking the Thames marshes. A specific study of place-names in this area[130] shows that they belong to the earliest phase of Saxon settlement; the general name for the area seems to have been *fenn ge* – now Vange – meaning 'marsh district'. The element –ge– in place-names is a very archaic one indicating a distinct district, or *regio* (as Bede terms it).[131] These *regiones* – Vange, Dengie, and *Ginge* are the three known in Essex – were probably tribal statelets in existence before the kingdom of the East Saxons.[132] The Vange peninsula formed a distinct bloc of land during the Roman occupation,[133] many of the features of which have survived to the present day. As the whole area between the Mar Dyke and Vange Creek is known from archaeological evidence (see entry on Mucking) to have been an entry point for some of the first Saxon migrants, it is possible that these new settlers lost no time in taking over intact the administration of a Roman *pagus* or local government district.

Location: St Mary's Church is in Church Road, Corringham, at the end of a cul-de-sac. It can be approached from the north on the B1420 which runs off the A13. This is called Southend Road at its northern end, and it then becomes Lampits Hill. The southern approach is by The Manorway, the A1014, a dual carriageway running from the A13 into the oil refineries at Coryton. Turn off it at the B1420. The nearest station is Stanford-le-Hope, about 3 km distant. The church is normally kept locked; for access apply to the rector on 0375 673074.

Danbury

Earliest known form of name: **Danengeberiam** 1086 (DB)
Derivation: the stronghold of the Daen(n)ingas

> Danbury, midway between Chelmsford and Maldon, stands in a
> delightful position on a hill of the same name, commanding one of
> the most beautiful landscapes in Essex. The crest of the hill is
> surrounded by the remains of the ancient camp or earthwork,
> within which the village is enclosed, the church (St John Baptist)
> standing on the summit, its lofty spire forming a conspicuous
> landmark for miles around.

So wrote the ecclesiologist Worley in 1915,[134] and the view from
Danbury is still as beautiful. Indeed, Danbury for long claimed to be
the highest point in Essex;[135] its summit at 110 m, however, is
exceeded, by 29 m, by High Wood in the parish of Elmdon, but the
prospect over the Chelmer Valley from this eminence is certainly
striking and picturesque – on a clear day the hills of Kent can be seen
beyond the silver Thames.

It was on this hill that Iron Age men first built a fort, perhaps as a
citadel against riverborne invaders.[136] And after the end of Roman
occupation Danbury was refortified against a new threat, one of three
hillforts in Essex known to have been re-occupied (see separate
entries on Asheldham and Downham). A sherd of Roman pottery was
sealed beneath the rebuilt rampart, proving its post-Roman date, and
Saxon pottery also found dated from the seventh century.

From its name, Danbury was the 'stronghold of the Daenningas',
and in early Saxon Essex it may have been the centre or retreat of a
semi-independent group of settlers. The Daenningas (meaning
'dwellers in the woodland'?) also gave their name to the marshy
Dengie peninsula and to the now-vanished *Danegris*, the wood of the
Daenningas, which formerly stretched from the Crouch to Danbury,
screening and further isolating the peninsula. In a charter of the East
Saxon King Suebred dating from between 706 and 709, reference is
made to the *regio* of *Deningei*. The use of this term is significant; it
occurs not only in charters but also in Bede and other early literary
sources, and it is believed to reflect a very early state in the
development of the Anglo-Saxon kingdoms.[137] The Anglo-Saxon
equivalent term was –*ge*–, and it seems likely that the later and better-
known 'Heptarchy' kingdoms coalesced out of such early statelets. In
Dengie, as in the Thurrock peninsula (another postulated statelet), it

has been shown that a rectilinear Roman field and road pattern has largely survived 'probably due in part at least to the post-Roman integrity of the area'.[138]

The outline of the Danbury fort can still be traced, and the views alone reward the stroll. The parish church – which is well worth a visit in its own right – stands at the centre of the fort, the site of the northern ramparts being marked by the main road. From the Griffin Inn, go into the churchyard and follow the footpath on the left-hand side which follows the boundary of the large house called Frettons. A spectacular vista emerges to the south. The rampart curves round to the right, skirting the edge of the housing development in South Hill Close etc. A path takes the visitor across allotments to the western side, where a line of trees stands on a marked rise. The rest of the rampart remains are on private land, curving round the rectory and back to the main road.

Location: Danbury lies on the A414 halfway between Chelmsford and Maldon. There is a large grassed parking area in front of the church.

Downham
Earliest known form of name: **Dunham** 1168
Derivation: enclosure on a hill

Here is a spot with one of the most spectacular views in Essex. The village of Downham stands on top of a steep (for Essex!) scarp of land running from Billericay across to Rettendon, looking down into the Crouch Valley. This high ground is really the tail end of a scarp running right across south Essex, marching across the county to Havering-atte-Bower, also renowned for its views, and, after being cut by the Roding and the Lea, ending up at Epping Forest. A driver travelling along the A127 from Gidea Park to Basildon will have this high ground to the north, dotted with churches, along the whole route.

Here at Downham Grange, an Iron Age fort was constructed to defend the area against the threat of seaborne or riverborne attack.[139] The fort's defences are to the south-west, north-east and east, showing from which direction assault was expected. Many hundreds of years passed: Roman invaders conquered yet abandoned the island in due course, and new settlers came. These new Germanic peoples – the Saxons – found the fort at Downham Grange, realized its potential and re-occupied it, just as they had done at Asheldham and

Danbury.[140] Nothing remains today of their fort, but its superb strategic siting is still all too obvious to the visitor.

Location: Downham Grange is a *private residence*, and the road to it is private as well. The panorama is best seen from Downham church (normally kept locked). This church stands on the central ridge of a triple spur of land. There is a large parking area next to the church from which the view over south Essex can be admired. To the right is the western spur, topped by Rectory Wood, and curving away to the left is the eastern spur on which sits Downham Grange. Downham church is reached from the A129 (London Road), up Castledon Road (this strangely fitting name is known only from 1777), signposted to Downham. The nearest station is Wickford. For those approaching on foot, turn right out of Wickford station into the High Street, then right into London Road. Castledon Road is about 1 km on the right. The church is about 2 km up the hill.

East Mersea

Earliest known form of name: **Meres ig(e)** 895 (ASC)
Derivation: island of the pool

Alfred the Great's desperate struggle against Danish invaders in the final decades of the ninth century received a fillip when, after regaining control of Wessex, he concluded a treaty with the Danish king of East Anglia, Guthrum, in the year 886. The peace that followed gave Alfred a breathing space to fortify the core of his kingdom and prepare for reconquest. However, in 892, the peace was broken, not by Guthrum, but by a new Danish raiding army which crossed from France in search of fresh booty. A succession of camps was established from which deep raids into the hinterland were made. A camp at Benfleet was destroyed in 893 (see separate entry for South Benfleet), and a new camp was built at Shoebury, probably abandoned by 895 (see separate entry for South Shoebury).

From Shoebury camp the Danes, under their leader Haesten, undertook a bold sortie as far as Chester and Wales. After overwintering in Wales the force returned in the summer of 894 to Essex, where they set up a temporary camp on Mersea Island. By the autumn they had abandoned this camp and moved their ships to the River Lea, where Alfred almost caught them by diverting the course of the river. The raiders marched across country to Bridgnorth and dispersed at last in 896.

Can any trace now be found of that Mersea camp occupied in the summer of 894? A tentative, though so far the only, suggestion as to its location was made as long ago as 1907.[141]

East Mersea church stands beside the partially moated Hall Farm, and in 1907 Gould speculated that the church and hall were once entirely surrounded by the moat. The site may therefore have been a defended Saxon settlement which could have been seized by Haesten's army. It should be said, however, that although Mersea was only a temporary camp, it was uncharacteristic of the Danes to pick an inland site, and even Gould had to admit that it was more likely that the camp was situated on the coast and has now been eroded away.

Between 1870–81 the parish church of St Edmund, East Mersea, was under the rectorship of Sabine Baring-Gould, a prominent Victorian hymn-writer, folklorist, historian and novelist. Although he disliked Mersea Island and its inhabitants during his stay, he immortalized the area in his stirring novel *Mehalah*, an Essex *Lorna Doone* and *Wuthering Heights* rolled into one. The interior of this mainly fourteenth-century church has modern pews and an open airy aspect, heightened by the dainty aisle piers. To the east of the church stands Hall Farm and beyond it (on private land) what remains of the moat. Gould believed that this moat had once extended southward on the other side of the farm buildings there, and that it had then turned north to follow Church Lane. There is certainly a dyke beside Church Lane which can be followed for some distance before it branches off to the west. Gould thought that this branch had formerly joined up again with the main part of the moat, completing the circle. There is no embanking or other surviving defensive arrangement, though the church and hall are on the slope of a low rise, and the surviving dyke seems hardly large enough to have once been a defensive moat.

Location: The church and hall lie in Church Lane off East Mersea Road. Take the B1025 from Colchester, and bear left at the fork immediately after crossing The Strood. The church is normally kept open.

East Tilbury

Earliest known form of name: **Tilaburg** *c.* 735 (Bede)
Derivation: the *burh* of Tila

And when Cedd had been raised to the dignity of bishop, he returned to his province [i.e. Essex] and used his increased authority to promote the work already begun. He built churches in several places and ordained priests and deacons to assist in teaching the faith and baptizing the people, especially in the city which the Saxons call Ythancaestir and that called Tilaburg.[142]

So Bede described Tilbury's place in the re-conversion of the East Saxons, in the year 653. Ythancaestir was the Roman fort of *Othona* at Bradwell-on-Sea (see separate entry), but where exactly was Bede referring to when he mentioned the 'city of Tilaburg'?

Some authorities prefer the elevated site of St James, West Tilbury, on the basis of earthworks surrounding that church,[143] or the fact that an eighth-century Saxon font was discovered there[144] (now in East Tilbury church). However, other writers plump for East Tilbury, usually on the grounds that it lies at the end of a Roman road,[145] itself on the route of an ancient trackway to a Thames crossing.

Topographically and archaeologically, East Tilbury has the better claim. It stands on a site superficially similar to *Othona*; it occupies a strategic headland surrounded by marsh, it is remote but joined to higher ground by a Roman road, and there are substantial Roman remains in the area. Unfortunately, unlike *Othona*, we cannot yet be sure of the exact nature of the Roman site at East Tilbury. There is much evidence of it, however; circular huts, probably Romano-British, used to be visible on the foreshore, where a great deal of pottery has also been found. There is Roman brick in the church and eighteenth-century gravel-digging near the church uncovered fragments of tessellated pavement.[146] Pottery is still being discovered in the Coalhouse Fort area.[147] Roofing tiles and hypocaust tiles have also been found, indicating that 'A substantial Roman building certainly exists in the area of St Catherine's Church'.[148]

Furthermore, in the Middle Ages East Tilbury was known as Great Tilbury, indicating that it was the more important of the two. Nothing now remains of Cedd's Saxon chapel, though it may have survived into the medieval period as the Hospital of St Mary. This was built – perhaps from the stones of Cedd's chapel – in 1213 on land belonging to a man with the significant name of Clement de Monasterio. The hospital stood near the site of Coalhouse Fort, at Coalhouse Point. Later in the Middle Ages the hospital declined to a free chapel or chantry; this chapel was, after its dissolution in 1536, directly converted into a blockhouse to defend the Thames.[149] This, however, quickly fell into disrepair; a map of 1735 shows the blockhouse in ruins and the sea encroaching upon the old sea wall which protected it. Today Coalhouse Point can be reached on foot through the municipal park surrounding Coalhouse Fort; in front of a disused battery, the saltings curve out into the river, almost to the point where the chapel/blockhouse once stood. The bleak river scene, here at what has always been the lowest regular crossing of the Thames (across to Higham in Kent), is now somewhat industrialized. Still, however, the mind turns back a millennium and a half, to imagine Cedd arriving in his boat here on this windswept shore, to begin again the task of converting the rugged and independent East Saxon folk of the hinterland.

Overlooking Coalhouse Fort on higher ground is the flint-walled church of St Catherine, the present-day parish church. St Catherine's is Norman, enlarged in the twelfth century, with a thirteenth-century chancel. From here, the visitor can look across to the fort and river beyond. In the chancel lies an eleventh-century Saxon font, graceful in its functional simplicity. The font stood originally in West Tilbury church where it was used to baptize Essex children from before Edward the Confessor's day until about 1880, when a new font was provided.[150]

At West Tilbury the striking hilltop church is now redundant. Here a large stone vessel was discovered half buried in the grounds of West Tilbury Hall by local historian E.A. Loftus. With some difficulty, because of its great weight, the crudely shaped vessel, 860 mm in diameter and 480 mm high, was dug up and moved to the churchyard. It is believed to have been an eighth-century immersion font,[151] and it formerly stood in the angle between the tower and the porch. However, it is no longer on site, and the church has been converted into a private residence.

Location: East Tilbury church lies at the end of Princess Margaret Road, which branches off the old A13 (now A1013) as Buckingham Hill Road; this can be reached from the Stanford-le-Hope A13 interchange. Follow signs to Coalhouse Fort. By train, East Tilbury station is 2 km distant. The church is open, with teas served, on the last Sunday of each month. There is ample parking at the nearby Coalhouse Fort, with which a visit can be combined. The site of the chapel/blockhouse is in the saltings off Coalhouse Point, which can be reached on foot across the municipal park. The Point lies behind a disused concrete building which lies south-west of the fort.

Faulkbourne: see entry for White Notley

Fobbing

Earliest known form of name: **Fobbinge** 1086 (DB)
Derivation: Fobba's creek[152]

Fobbing's greatest claim to fame is that it was the birthplace of the Peasants' Revolt. In 1381 men from Fobbing refused to co-operate with a census which would lead to a poll tax being levied against them. They rose up after the tax commissioner for the area tried to have them arrested, and widespread violence followed throughout south Essex, eventually leading to Wat Tyler's famous march on London. This event is commemorated by a controversial sculpture erected by Thurrock District Council on Fobbing's recreation ground.

Our interest in Fobbing, however, lies at the parish church of St Michael, where Saxons left their mark centuries before John Ball dreamt of liberty. Like Corringham, Fobbing stands on a gravel hill overlooking the Thames marshes, and quite a prominent hill it is too, a plainly visible landmark from anywhere in the marshes or out on the river. It is also a fine vantage point for looking down on to Fobbing and Corringham Marshes, now covered by the oil refineries of Coryton and Shellhaven. To the east lie Vange Creek and Canvey Island, while inland the Langdon Hills can be seen.

St Michael's – the dedication of so many hilltop churches – dates mainly from the fourteenth and fifteenth century. It has a prominent tower at the west end, which is certainly of the fifteenth century, but the nave itself was originally built by Saxon hands in the eleventh century;[153] the only substantial part of the Saxon nave to survive is the north wall, only 75 cms thick. In this wall a blocked double-splayed Saxon round-headed window can be seen from both inside and outside. A visit to this church can be combined easily with one to Corringham nearby to compare the Saxon workmanship of each.

Location: The village of Fobbing can be reached either from the A13, turning off at the Five Bells roundabout into Fobbing High Road (signposted to Fobbing), or from the south by turning off the A1014 Manorway into Corringham's Church Road and then taking the third right, Fobbing Road, which leads into Fobbing High Road. The church lies at the end of the High Road, and it should be possible to park outside. The church is normally kept closed; for access contact the rector on 0375 672002.

Great Canfield

Earliest known form of name: **Canedfeldam** 1086 (DB)
Derivation: *Cana*'s open country

Most visitors to the lovely parish church of St Mary come to see the fine thirteenth-century wall-painting depicting the Virgin and Child, which is situated behind the altar. As Pevsner notes, it is 'one of the best thirteenth-century representations of the subject in the whole country, full of tenderness.' When we visited the church an American couple were drooling over the painting and photographing it from every angle, unaware that above their heads was a piece of art two centuries older, created even before the Normans built this flint-walled church. This pre-Norman treasure is literally a hidden gem.

The church is entered through a Norman doorway with very exotic carvings – a face with two birds pecking at it and a zigzag pattern. Once through the door, one of the most striking features is the chancel arch. The topmost part of the pillar supporting the arch, usually in the form of a capital or moulding upon which the foot of the arch rests, is known as an impost. At Great Canfield, the impost on the south side of the chancel arch contains a piece of worked stone re-used by the Normans. The upper face of the stone contains an Anglo-Danish carving from the early eleventh century. This stone appears to have been a grave slab originally. Most of the stone is hidden by later masonry, but on the lower part an elaborately carved though indeterminate 'beast' can be seen, amid intricate scrollwork. Fortunately it can be seen, by dint of a very large pole with a mirror attached, kept in the church for the purpose; it would otherwise be quite inaccessible!

Location: Great Canfield is one of those good-old scattered Essex villages with 'ends' stretching from Great Dunmow down to The Rodings and across to Takeley on the A120. Church End is situated on a minor road off the B184, the Roman road to Dunmow. Just north of High Roding a signposted lane leads to Church End; St Mary's appears on the right after about a kilometre. There is a wide verge for parking and the church is normally kept open. The Norman motte and bailey of Great Canfield Castle, built by the de Veres, can be seen from the churchyard.

Great Hallingbury

Earliest known form of name: **Halingeb(er)iam** 1086 (DB)
Derivation: the *burh* of Healla's people

As noted by Reaney, the *burh*, or defended site, referred to in the place-name was probably the nearby prehistoric fort of Wallbury. That the fort was some particular Saxon group's *burh*, implies re-use of that fort of course; Wallbury was a very large fort, over 300 m from ditch to ditch on its north-south axis, but unfortunately archaeology has not been able to confirm such re-use.

Great Hallingbury's parish church, St Giles, is a prominent landmark for motorists on the M11, its tall spire visible to the east between junctions 7 and 8. Apart from the chancel arch, which we will come to shortly, the oldest structural part of the building is the tower, which is of the fourteenth century. The rest of the church was ruthlessly modernized in 1874 by the then lord of the manor, J. Archer Houblon. But a quick look at the Victorian exterior does not prepare the visitor for what lies inside. As Pevsner notes, 'Internally, however, to one's surprise, one finds a complete Early Norman chancel-arch built up entirely of Norman bricks'.[154]

The chancel arch is indeed the most striking feature of the interior, but opinion divides over whether the ever-cautious Pevsner was correct in his view that this feature was Norman. The little guidebook on sale in the church follows him, and calls the arch late eleventh-century.[155] Worley is equivocal – the arch is either late Saxon or early Norman[156] – as is Mee, who says 'it was made about the time the Normans came'.[157] Scarfe is more positive, and definitely calls it late Saxon.[158] Perhaps it is safest to say: visitor, go and see for yourself; this arch, built from the bricks of a vanished age, itself spans two ages.

Location: Great Hallingbury lies about 2½ km south-east of Bishop's Stortford (nearest railway station). Motorists can approach it from junction 8 of the M11. Take the A120 Dunmow Road then an almost immediate right signposted to Great Hallingbury. This bears right in due course into the village. The approach from Bishop's Stortford station is, right out of the station onto the A1060 Hallingbury Road for about 2 km, then left at Church Road, signposted to Great Hallingbury. The church and village are 2 km further on, over the M11. There is no parking directly outside the church but there is a rough layby a short distance to the west on the other side of the road. The church is normally kept locked; for access contact the priest-in-charge on 0279 72334.

Great Leighs

Earliest known forms of name: **Lega, Legram** 1086 (DB)
Derivation: the Saxon word *leah* means 'a clearing in a wood' when it occurs in a cluster of place-names, but when it is isolated, as in this case, it means 'wood' or 'meadow'[159]

St Mary's Church possesses one of only six round towers in Essex. The origins of the tower are obscure but, though built or at least heavily restored by the Normans, it was reputedly Saxon in origin. However, the Saxon fabric now survives only in the foundations or the base of the tower. Historical notes pinned up in the church porch give the date of the Saxon tower's construction as AD 970, though we do not know on what authority this rests. There is a fine Norman doorway in the base of the tower, with typical zigzag patterning. The spire was added in the 1880s.

There has been much discussion about the reason for round church towers, which are very rare in our county, though 160 survive in Norfolk and Suffolk.[160] One theory is that in the absence of freely available local stone which could be squared, it was easier to build flint walls up in a circular fashion. Less plausibly, it has also been claimed that they were defensive structures used as lookout posts from which to spot Viking invaders, or shelter from them.[161] Certainly none of the round-towered churches in Essex date back that far.

Location: Great Leighs lies on the A131 halfway between Chelmsford and Braintree. The church, however, is a considerable distance out of the village, well past even Church End, over the infant River Ter and nearly opposite the 500-year-old Lyons Hall. To get to the church from the village, turn off at the St Anne's Castle pub, rather implausibly claimed to be the oldest licensed public house in England – and haunted – by the historical notes in the church porch, and continue on this lane for about 4 km. The church is normally kept locked; for access contact the rector on 0245 361218.

Great Stambridge

Earliest known form of name: **Stanbruge** 1086 (DB)
Derivation: stone bridge

The pretty church of St Mary and All Saints looks out over gently sloping fields to the Roach. Beyond stand the tower blocks of Southend-on-Sea, but this corner of Essex between Crouch and Roach is still rural and relatively isolated. There is a fine tower, mainly fifteenth-century, with much later brick battlements, and a dainty white-painted flèche which once served as a mark for shipping. But this church has been a landmark for a millennium, for in the nave and chancel we find traces of Saxon work. This Saxon church, built about 1020–40, was a double-celled structure familiar in ecclesiastical buildings of this period.

The nave's north wall, built from ragstone and pudding-stone, is pre-Norman, and high in the chancel is the outline of a pre-Conquest window arch. The nave wall has a curious off-set or step about halfway up, and a double row of pudding-stones form the footings for further blocked windows, which are also outlined by large pudding-stones. Further massive blocks of pudding-stones at the west end of the nave, particularly on the south side of the tower, are also examples of Saxon fabric, and Mee suggested[162] that the tower itself was Saxon 'as high as the arm can reach'.

In the adjacent parish of Canewdon a curious and monumental stone statue was dug up in the nineteenth century in a field at Pudsey Hall. A contemporary account of it was given by Rochford Hundred historian Philip Benton:

> Part of a gigantic statue, supposed to represent a heathen deity, was dug up upon Pudsey-Hall in 1847. It is still in existence, and lies in the yard near the house. It was found in a field called Great Hydes (adjoining Hyde Wood), on the south side of the road leading from Canewdon to Ashingdon. A head of a battle-axe was found near, said to have been a Norman weapon. Beneath the statue were appearances of bones, which crumbled upon exposure to air.[163]

Although this object was probably Romano-British or prehistoric, at least one writer has speculated that the statue was a Saxon representation of a god, perhaps Thor as Thundersley lies nearby.[164] Unfortunately we will never know, as the statue was broken up for hard core by the farmer.

Location: Great Stambridge church lies about 2 km east of Rochford (nearest station), and can be reached by following East Street from the town centre. East Street then becomes Stambridge Road. The church lies on a sharp bend in the road and there is ample parking on a large grassy area in front of the church. Great Stambridge village is about 1 km further on along the Stambridge Road. The church is normally kept open, though the fabric is concealed in the interior by whitewashed rendering.

Great Tey
Earliest known forms of name: (at) **Tygan, Tigan** *c.* 950
Derivation: *tiege*, a variant of the more usual *teag*, an enclosure

As massive as a castle, St Barnabas Church stands in the middle of a large open green, in effect its churchyard. There are some fine timbered buildings around the green, but the eye is first drawn to the great tower, 6 m square, which rises up in four stages above the village. This tower is tenth century[165] and built with much Roman brick. The battlemented topmost stage, which houses the bells, is Norman. Beneath, the third stage has two broad round-headed windows in each face. Below the windows in each face is an arcade of six blind round-headed recesses. At the lowest level are two plainer round-headed windows.

The sheer size of the church led Pevsner to wonder why the small village of Great Tey should have had such a magnificent building erected.[166] But the church we see today is considerably smaller than when first built. The church was originally cruciform, but in 1829 when the church was in poor repair, the cost of renovation was put at £700. To save money, all but one bay of the nave on the north side of the church and the east and west transepts were demolished – but the cost of demolition came to £1,400![167] The chancel was converted into the nave and further restoration left the church interior looking rather plain, in contrast to the rich and dominating exterior.

Location: Great Tey lies about 10 km west of Colchester on Brook Road, a minor road between the A120 and A604. Nearest stations are Chappel & Wakes Colne, about 3 km to the north, and Marks Tey, about 5 km to the south-east. The church is usually kept open.

Greensted
Earliest known form of name: **Gernestedam** 1086 (DB)
Derivation: the green place

Over two centuries ago the father of Essex history, Philip Morant, wrote of Greensted church, 'It is a very uncommon antique building, for the walls are of timber, not framed, but trees split, or sawn asunder, and set into the ground.'[168]

In the quiet churchyard, dwarfed by massive cypress trees, St Andrew's still stands, a unique treasure in Essex and in all England. This church is the only surviving Saxon timber building anywhere.

The Saxon nave is made of oak tree trunks, dated by dendrochronological analysis to AD 845.[169] The tree trunks were split vertically into three, the outer slabs made into a palisade wall, each slab dovetailed into its neighbour, and the central, heartwood planks used for sills and roof timbers. There are twenty-eight logs on the north wall, including three extra squared pieces of timber filling a space where a door once stood, and twenty-one logs remaining on the south wall. There are two further corner posts, and ten logs in the west wall partly obscured by the tower. Of these timbers, only about thirty-five are original in their present position.[170] Not a nail was used in the construction, the logs being held together with timber pins.

The original building would have been thatched and almost windowless; the scorch-marks of the Saxon torches used to light the interior can still be seen. The weatherboarded tower with its shingled spire is of uncertain date, but the brick chancel and dormer windows are Tudor additions. Excavations in 1960, and subsequently, discovered a succession of older, wooden chancels of uncertain date. Thorough restoration in 1848 saw the insertion of new sills and a brick plinth under the logs, which had to be shortened as they had rotted so badly.

Greensted church is inextricably linked with the cult of St Edmund. Edmund, king of East Anglia, was martyred by Danish invaders in 869. His veneration as a saint was already under way within a quarter of a century, and tales of miracles soon arose with his cult. He quickly became one of the most popular saxon saints. The oak tree at Hoxne in Suffolk where he was traditionally shot full of arrows survived until the middle of the last century and, after it had fallen, 'Edmund's Tree' was found to contain a Danish arrowhead embedded in the tree trunk. A wooden-bound bible and prayer book in the possession of Greensted church is made from the timbers of that tree.

After his death, Edmund's body was brought to London for safety, but in 1013 it was decided to return the remains to Bury St Edmunds. Both these events have been suggested as the origin of Greensted church, which could have begun life as a temporary resting place for St Edmund's body *en route*. Against this tradition, however, is the very substantial nature of the original construction, which is far too solid to have been a temporary erection. However, there seems every reason to accept the persistent tale that the church did provide shelter for St Edmund's body, in 1013 at least.

The interior of the church has great charm and venerable serenity. Fillets cover the timber joints, giving an effect like rich panelling to the inner faces of the logs, where the rough adze marks of the Saxon carpenters can still be seen. A small painted wooden panel hangs in the nave, probably from a fifteenth-century rood-screen. This panel shows Edmund in the act of being martyred, crowned but clad only in a loincloth, tied to a tree and being shot full of arrows. A fragment of ancient glass in one of the dormer windows depicts a crowned man's head, also said to represent St Edmund.

Location: Greensted church lies on the Greensted Road leading from Chipping Ongar, which is at the junction of the B184 from Great Dunmow, the A113 from Chigwell, and the A414 Chelmsford–Harlow 'Trans-Essex Highway'. Ongar lies at the end of the London Underground's Central Line, and the church is also on the Essex Way long-distance footpath. Greensted is about 2 km from the station; turn right into the High Street and then turn into Banson's Lane to follow the Essex Way or continue south to turn right at The Borough, which becomes Greensted Road. There is ample parking and the church is normally kept open.

Hadstock

Earliest known form of name: **Caddanno** 1008, later **Hadestoc** *c.* 1200
Derivation: Caddanho means 'Cada's spur of land', Hadstock means 'Hada's or Headda's enclosed settlement'

The church of St Botolph, Hadstock, stands on sloping ground overlooking an unspoilt village. The first impression is one of great scale, a bulky yet graceful church for such a small village. A holy well dedicated to St Botolph once stood here,[171] perhaps indicating a pagan origin to Christian worship on this hilltop site. The Anglo-Saxon origins of the church have been known for some time, but a systematic study including excavations from 1974–9 has shown a building sequence more complex than previously supposed.[172]

In the middle Saxon period the first church was built. It was similar in size and plan to the present church, and had a nave, choir, and apsidal chancel, with a *porticus* (side chapel) extending on each side of the choir. Later in the Anglo-Saxon period the central choir had a timber-framed tower added to it and the nave was re-aligned to make it skew. A number of Saxon churches are deliberately out of true, including Chickney (see separate entry); this feature is believed to represent Christ's skewed body on the cross. A doorway was also inserted at the western end of the north wall.

At the end of the Anglo-Saxon period the church was again rebuilt. A new masonry tower was erected in place of the timber one, with monumental masonry supporting it. A new doorway (the present one) was inserted in the north wall to replace the older one. The Saxon tower collapsed in the thirteenth century, and a new tower was built at the west end in the fifteenth century; the church underwent further alterations, including 'restoration' on a drastic scale in the 1880s, when the present chancel, vestry and organ chamber were built.

It has been suggested[173] that the church may be the monastery and last resting place of St Botolph. Traditionally the church was destroyed by the Danes in 870 and rebuilt, perhaps by Cnut if the Battle of Assandun was at Ashdon nearby rather than at Ashingdon (see separate entry). This traditional history fits well with the results of the archaeological investigation. St Botolph's monastery was founded at a desolate spot called *Icanho* in East Anglia in 654, and after his death in *c.* 680, he was buried there. The body was removed in the tenth century and distributed to Ely, Thorney and Westminster. Just such a high status grave was found in the south *porticus* or transept during excavations, and the body or sarcophagus had indeed been later exhumed and the grave-space backfilled. Hadstock, earlier *Caddanho*, may therefore be identical with the lost site of *Icanho*. The rebuild of the church does seem to have been as a result of a serious fire, perhaps caused by Danes. The late Saxon rebuild is also difficult to explain unless it was externally imposed; could this be Cnut's minster built to commemorate victory at Assandun? For reasons given elsewhere (see entry on Ashingdon) we do not believe Assandun was fought at Ashdon, but the rebuild then becomes a mystery, unless the district suddenly grew very wealthy from some unknown circumstances.

What remains to be seen today of the successive Anglo-Saxon churches at Hadstock? From the exterior we can see the oldest parts of the church – the nave walls. These date from that first, middle Saxon church, perhaps Botolph's minster, and are original up to about half their present height. The lower courses of the north *porticus* or transept also date from this period. Passing through the fifteenth-century porch, we come to a fine doorway which is itself Saxon, though reconstructed in medieval times. The massive door in front of us is also Saxon; as Mee vividly puts it, 'Had the Conqueror come this way, he would have found it swinging on its hinges'.[174] This door is one of only two known Saxon doors in the whole country – the other is also in Essex, at Buttsbury (see separate entry). This great oak door has three iron straps riveted through it; under one of these straps was found a piece of 'Daneskin' now on display at Saffron Walden Museum and scientifically proven to be human skin (see discussion under entry for Ashingdon). The west jamb of the doorway has some interesting 'palmette' ornamentation.

Above this doorway is a blocked Saxon window, one of five which survive of the original six. They all are characteristically narrow and double-splayed. They still have their original Saxon timber frames, and parts of the roof timbers are also Saxon. The entrance into the north *porticus* or transept is marked by Saxon jambs. One has a plinth with palmette-ornamented capitals like the doorway. On the south side, the Saxon plinths revealed by the excavation have been left exposed. Through the archway the south transept contained the high-status body referred to above, perhaps the tomb of St Botolph himself.

Location: Hadstock is one of Essex's northernmost parishes. It lies about 10 km north of Saffron Walden on the B1052, which joins the A604 about 2 km to the north at Linton, now in Cambridgeshire, but once partly in Essex. There is a large grassed parking area by the churchyard. The church is normally kept open, and there is an excellent guidebook summarizing the results of the excavations.[175]

Harlow
Earliest known form of name: (at) **Herlawe** 1045
Derviation: army hill

The only prominent hill in Harlow is the one near the River Stort in the Temple Fields Industrial Estate; this hill has been a centre for religious activity at least since the Iron Age,[176] but is best known for its Roman temple which is marked out in outline. Excavation has also revealed that when the Roman temple fell into ruins, early Saxon settlers built a timber building, probably a shrine, though no trace of it now remains. Another Saxon timber building lies under Harlowbury Chapel (1 km to the south-east). If this hill ('Stanegrovehelle' in the fourteenth century meaning 'Stone-ditch hill') was the 'army hill' which gave Harlow its name, it was presumably of military importance because of its strategic position overlooking a great bend in the Stort, and because it stood beside the Roman river-crossing of the road between Bishop's Stortford and Chigwell (*Durolitum*).

Nearby in Old Harlow, however, is a tumulus which gave its name to the vicinity. The modern form of the name is Mulberry Green, but it was earlier Mudborow, which may derive from Anglo-Saxon *(ge)mot beorh*, meaning 'the moot' or 'meeting place of the hundred'.[177] This tumulus may thus mark the hundred's place of assembly, though the temple hill has also been proposed for that honour,[178] and indeed this, rather than the temple hill, may be the 'army hill' which gave Harlow its name.

A short distance from the tumulus is Harlowbury Chapel, now an ancient monument and standing in fields on Harlow's outskirts. It is looked after by the Friends of Harlowbury Chapel, and inside there is an exhibition about its history, though chiefly about its use as a granary in more recent times. Most authorities give this chapel a twelfth-century date on stylistic grounds, including the little guidebook available in the chapel which notes,

> The chapel has datable features ascribed to the late 12th century, notably the carved stone waterleaf capitals of the north doorway and the rounded windows of dressed stone . . . However recent archaeological investigation of the floor revealed evidence of an earlier timber structure which suggests there was a chapel on the site from Saxon times.[179]

Recently, however, an interesting and controversial theory has been advanced. Hewett and Taylor make the following suggestion:

> The chapel at Harlowbury appears at first sight to be wholly of Norman and later date, on the evidence of its windows and doorway which would suit a date in the last quarter of the twelfth century. But we believe that these Norman features of dressed stone are later insertions into an earlier unbuttressed rectangular building of rough rubble and tile.[180]

Surviving elements of typically later Saxon roof fittings in the fabric have led them to this conclusion, which is similar to that in two other Saxon buildings, St Martin's, Canterbury and Sompting church in West Sussex.

At Harlow's museum in Passmore House, the Local History Room 2 contains some Saxon finds from the area. The 'Saxon Harlow' cabinet contains part of a cooking pot, a silver coin of Offa from Little Hallingbury, and a Saxon arrowhead, as well as information about the pre-Norman origins of Harlowbury Chapel.

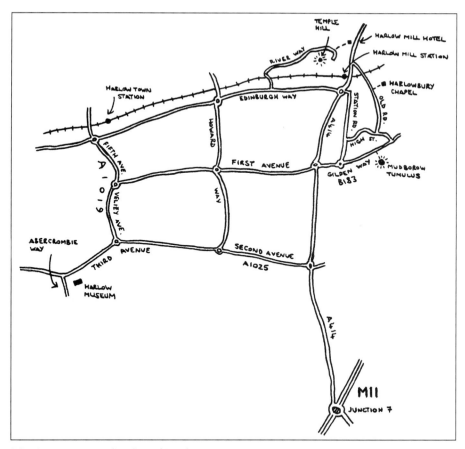

The Saxon sites and sights of Harlow

Location: The temple hill lies beside River Way, in the middle of the Temple Fields Industrial Estate. River Way is off Edinburgh Way. If approaching on foot it is best via the A11 from Harlow Hill Station, and then along the footpath beside the Harlow Mill Hotel, turning off to the left into the industrial estate.

The Mudborow tumulus lies on a footpath running south from Gilden Way, Old Harlow. There is no parking in this area and Gilden Way is a busy road. It is best to park or start from Sheering Village, then walk along Gilden Way, past Sheering Drive and the tumulus is a short distance down the second footpath on the left.

Harlowbury Chapel is situated off Old Road, Harlow; there is a signposted footpath across the fields. The chapel itself stands on *private ground*, and is normally kept locked. Visitors are welcome to walk round the exterior of the chapel, and a look at the interior can be arranged by contacting 0279 29414, or see the notice on the door of the chapel.

Harlow Museum is at Passmores House, Third Avenue. Opening times: Monday, Wednesday, Friday to Sunday, 10 a.m. to 5 p.m., Tuesday and Thursday, 10 a.m. to 9 p.m. Closed 12.30 p.m. to 1.30 p.m., Saturday and Sunday.

Harrowdown, in the parish of Birdbrook

Earliest known form of name: **Harewe** fourteenth century
Derivation: hill of the pagan shrine

The parish of Birdbrook is at the very top end of Essex, abutting the Stour and looking across into Suffolk. Its highest point is Harrowdown, with a triangulation point at the top, 92 m above sea-level. This prominent hill has a commanding view over the Stour Valley, and it is not surprising that it attracted pagan Saxons to place a shrine here.[181] The site is one of six known pagan place-names in Essex.[182] The name of Harrow in Middlesex also derives from the Saxon word *hearg*, pagan temple or shrine; this Harrow lay, of

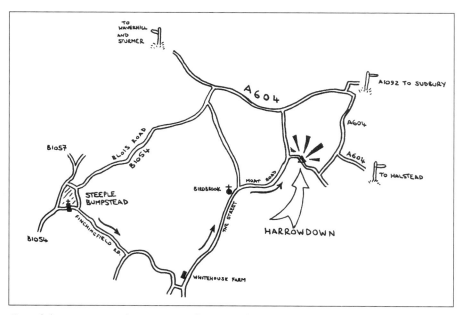

Site of the pagan temple at Harrowdown, in the parish of Birdbrook

following signs to Kelvedon. Parking in the vicinity of the church is difficult. The church is normally kept locked; for access contact the vicar on 0621 815434.

Little Bardfield

Earliest known form of name: **Birdefelda** 1086 (DB)
Derivation: this is a difficult place-name, but it probably means 'open land colonized by dependent peasants'

The Saxon church of St Katherine's, Little Bardfield, stands in a tranquil rural spot. Pigeons were cooing and crows clacking from the trees round about when we visited. Next door to the church stands Little Bardfield Hall, a spectacular 'Tudor' jettied hall with some fine pargeting on the gables. This Tudor front, however, is a fake, added in 1925 onto a fine Georgian portico – which had itself been added in the eighteenth century onto the front of an Elizabethan building!

The church's nave and tower are both pre-Conquest, probably dating from the reign of Edward the Confessor.[189] As the church guidebook puts it so dramatically,

> When this little church of St Katherine was built the lights of Saxon England were indeed going out for ever . . . this church was built before William the Conqueror dreamt of invading these shores.[190]

It is the tower which is the church's outstanding glory. This massive and striking monument to the architects of a millennium ago rises up in five stages. The tower is built mainly of flint and rubble, each stage divided from the next by a 'string-course' of rubble. The embattled parapet and spire are modern, but the narrow round-headed windows are original, as is the blocked western doorway. The nave is of the same date as the tower. There is some re-used Roman brick in the fabric and also 'clunch', locally available hard, dressed, chalk. But the use of so much flint at this early date is remarkable, particularly where it is used as a decoration around the doorways and window openings.[191] The north wall of the nave contains one blocked round-headed Saxon window at the eastern end, while in the south wall there is another blocked Saxon window, double-splayed like the first. This is now obscured by the porch and can only be seen from inside the church. The interior is plastered, so the fabric of the building is best viewed from outside.

Location: Little Bardfield is on the Bardfield Road between Thaxted and Great Bardfield. The church of St Katherine, which is at the western end of the village, is down a lane on the north side of Bardfield Road. There is a grassy area in front of the church for parking, and the church is normally kept open.

Magdalen Laver

Earliest known form of name: (aet) **Lagefare** *c.* 1010
Derivation: possibly 'passage of a stream'; a number of brooks associated with the Roding flow through the area

The little isolated church of St Mary Magdalene gave the village its name, and a very pretty church it is too. The church is Norman, and there is a charming (and typically Essex) wooden tower at the west end. This tower is sixteenth century; it has white weatherboarding at its base, then a tiled sloping roof topped by a small weatherboarded bell turret. However, the Norman church, built on a slight prominence, is founded on older, pagan, ground. Built into the foundations of the north wall are two large dark round pudding-stones, which are likely to have been foci for pagan worship before the arrival of Christianity. The building of the church over the stones represented the symbolic 'conquest' of paganism.

The stones were deliberately placed at the corners of the north wall, one at the bell tower end, one at the chancel end.[192] The grass grows richly around the church walls so the stones may not be easy to spot at first glance. There is also a very large and unexplained stone lying next to the east end of the chancel, nearly 2 m across and flattish.

Location: Magdalen Lever is a scattered hamlet about 6 km east of Harlow. There are no main roads in the area; it is best approached from the Tyler's Green roundabout of the A414. The church itself is at the end of a long lane which passes Hall Farm. The church is normally kept open, and there is a large parking area.

Maldon

Earliest known form of name: **Maeldune** 913 (ASC)
Derivation: hill marked by a cross

Alfred the Great's reign was followed by that of his son Edward the Elder, and Edward continued his father's task of ending Danish rule in England. The reconquest took much of his long reign, and was characterized by a careful strategy of building a network of forts – *burhs* – in the national heartland followed by steady advance into 'Danelaw', each captured area being also fortified in its turn. By 912 Edward had moved into Essex; in that year, the *Anglo-Saxon Chronicle* recorded that he camped at Maldon while the *burh* at Witham was being built. A *burh* at Maldon followed in 916; a determined Danish attack the following year was beaten off and Colchester was stormed and seized by the English, completing the conquest of Essex.

The Maldon *burh* was then an important 'forward base' which played a key role in the history of Essex. Does anything remain of it today? Recent archaeological and topographical study[193] has revealed fresh information about the boundaries of the *burh*.

The site is an ancient one. Present-day Maldon is situated on a strategic hill overlooking the Blackwater. Saltmaking has given this area an importance since prehistoric times, and it was certainly occupied in both the Iron Age and Roman periods; indeed, the Saxons may already have found a hillfort on this site which merely needed refurbishment.

The *burh* enclosed an area about 200 x 250 m, and formed a rough oval with London Road forming its main east-west axis. Visitors with an hour or so can roughly follow the circuit of the *burh* walls, although considerable imagination is required to envisage the defences along most of the route. Starting at the junction of London Road and Gate Street, there is a famous crack in a wall which marks the start of the circuit. The crack is in the garden wall of West House, opposite the extension at No. 9 London Road, and runs from top to bottom. This marks the easternmost point of the *burh*, which then turned north-west. Walk up Gate Street and turn left into Beeleigh Road. From here there are fine views over the river and surrounding countryside, the almost scarp-like slope giving some hint of the natural defensive position the *burh* occupied and the strategic value of its ramparts. West Chase marks the middle of the northern part of the circuit. At the end of Beeleigh Road, turn left into Dykes Chase, which marches with the western rampart of the *burh*. London Road cuts across our path and the wall then turns south-east, across the modern estate in Highlands Drive, before turning back at the southern end of Wellington Road (off London Road). Highland Drive extends round the grounds of St Peter's Hospital and then joins Spital Road. Here many of the properties have long rear gardens extending back to an earth bank, an ancient boundary which when excavated in 1985–6 proved to be part of the *burh* defences. Spital Road meets the eastern end of London Road.

About 1 km south-east of Maldon, between South House Farm and the causeway onto Northey Island, lies the spot where the renowned Battle of Maldon is believed to have been fought on 10 or 11 August 991. The fame of this battle stems largely from the Anglo-Saxon poem known as *The Battle of Maldon*. This tells the story of the battle in epic terms, and is one of the finest pieces of poetry in our history. The story of its survival is astonishing. It was preserved in a single manuscript in the Cotton Library, a private collection of historic documents. However, in 1731 the library caught fire and the original manuscript was completely destroyed. Very fortunately, the manuscript had been transcribed only six years before, and it is this reasonably accurate copy which survives today as our sole record of the poem.

Summarized very briefly, the poem tells the following tale. It opens with the men of the Essex militia making their way to Maldon. Once they had arrived at the causeway onto Northey Island, Byrhtnoth, the ealdorman of Essex, arranged them in battle order, to face the Vikings who were encamped on Northey Island. A Viking messenger was sent to demand tribute – but was given short shrift by Byrhtnoth. A battle was therefore inevitable, but the two sides could not immediately come to blows as the high tide had cut the island off. On the ebb, however, the Vikings tried to advance across the causeway but were blocked by three heroic men from the English side. The Vikings then demanded passage across the causeway so that there could be a fair fight, and Byrhtnoth, foolishly and over-confidently, let the hordes over. In the ferocious battle that followed, many were killed on both sides and Byrhtnoth himself was cut down. Once their leader was dead, many on the English side fled, leaving a heroic remnant to make a final stand and face inevitable death.

A small portion of the beginning and end of the poem are missing, but the sense remains clear. Enough independent records of the battle exist for confirmation of the general account given in the poem. There is a brief mention in the *Anglo-Saxon Chronicle*, including, in one version, the name of the Viking leader, Olaf Tryggvasson. The nearly contemporary *Vita Oswaldi* adds further details, and the twelfth-century chronicle of Florence of Worcester, probably relying on a now-lost version of the *Anglo-Saxon Chronicle*, adds other information. Also from the twelfth century is the *Liber Eliensis*, which gives a long account.

From these various, and often conflicting, accounts an idea can be drawn up of the accuracy of the poem. There was clearly a battle at a causeway on the 'Pante' (modern Blackwater), with the English forces, led by Byrhtnoth, being overwhelmed after Byrhtnoth's death. The Northey Island causeway is the most *plausible* site, but *proof* is lacking, not least because no finds have ever been made in the area. However, this may be because the battle was fought at a spot now under estuarine mud; geological research[194] has shown that the Southey Creek separating Northey from the mainland was much narrower in the tenth century, indeed less than half of its present width.

There is also ample proof that Byrhtnoth was a historical personage. He was ealdorman, or most senior nobleman, of Essex, and probably born about 930.[195] This would make him over sixty at the time of the battle – and he is described as tall and white-haired in the *Vita Oswaldi*. By the time of the Battle of Maldon, Byrhtnoth had risen in importance to become one of the most senior noblemen in England,[196] a close confidant of the king and owner of large estates. It is probably this high status that gave the Battle of Maldon an importance out of the ordinary; though it had little strategic significance, the fight was remembered as one in which a great leader had been cut down. The extent of his property can be traced from his wife's will; his holdings extend across the eastern counties, many being bequeathed by him to Ely Abbey.[197] It was to Ely Abbey where his body was carried for burial – headless as the Vikings had taken his head – and a tapestry depicting the battle was given to the abbey by his widow. When his tomb was opened in 1769 it was indeed found to contain a tall headless man with the collarbone almost cut through from a battle-axe or sword blow.[198]

Many other battle participants are named: the causeway guards Wulfstan, Maccus and Alfere; the nobleman Aelfwine; the warriors Offa and Leofsunu; the yeoman Dunnere; the Northumbrian hostage Aescferth; the traitors Godric, Godwine and Godwig. Some of the warriors can be plausibly identified with known Essex landowners (such as Leofsunu – see entry for Sturmer), though the commonness of their names precludes positive identification. Olaf Tryggvasson is believed to have been the Viking leader. Of royal descent, Olaf led at least one other devastating raid on England, and by force of arms created himself king of Norway in 995. His tactics were simple – strike ferociously and mercilessly with a very large army – and paid off; after ravaging southern England in 991 the raiding party left with £22,000 of gold and silver.

Much ink has been spilt on the question of the poem's accuracy. There seems little reason to doubt the main narrative, particularly where this leads the poet to criticize the hero, Byrhtnoth, for his pride.[199] Many of the battle scenes are, however, stylized; the poet uses stock phrases which occur in a number of Anglo-Saxon poems. The battle-speeches in particular are a familiar way in which heroism is expressed – such literary formulae date back to Classical times.[200] This use of standard literary motifs need not, however, invalidate the accuracy of the tale.

Discussion has also centred on the date of the poem's composition; a nearly contemporary account would have more 'eye-witness' value than one composed much later from a stock literary style. The use of certain supposedly anachronistic forms of language has persuaded some that the poem cannot have been written earlier than 1030,[201] though such arguments seem to have been comprehensively refuted.[202] *The Battle of Maldon* poem indeed seems to be a near-contemporary account of an incident in which great heroism was displayed against terrible odds. This is a familiar theme in English history, and one which still appeals today. The poem is still widely available, a lasting

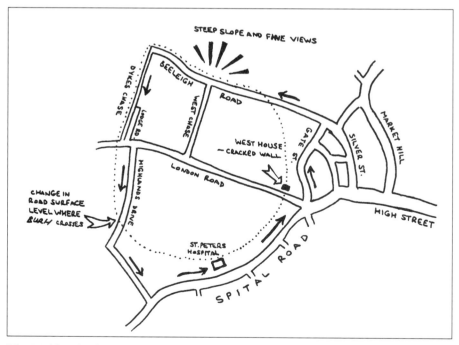

The Maldon *burh* trail. The dotted line shows the original position of the earthworks

tribute to the literary skill of the anonymous author and the ageless appeal of the ideals of selflessness, bravery and glory. We can be all the more proud that *The Battle of Maldon* commemorates East Saxon heroes whose names and deeds have not dimmed after a thousand years.

Location: Maldon lies at the end of the A414 from Chelmsford and can also be approached from the A12 via the B1018. Maldon is a busy town and parking can be difficult, particularly on Saturdays. The battle site lies about 2 km south-east of the town centre. It can be reached either via the B1018 southbound out of Maldon (Mundon Road), turning left into South House Chase (but parking is also limited here), or by walking along the riverside footpath at the Hythe, past the boating lake and the recreation ground. Northey Island is owned by the National Trust and maintained as a nature reserve. Visits are by appointment only; ring the warden on 0621 53142. The causeway is covered for four to five hours at each high tide.

Mucking
Earliest known form of name: **Muc(h)inga** 1086 (DB)
Derivation: Mucca's stream[203]

Today Mucking is a secluded hamlet, its houses and thirteenth-century church (now privately owned) standing near Mucking Creek. This stream flows into the Lower Hope, a strategic bend in the Thames at the lowest natural crossing point of the river which faces the widening mouth of the estuary proper.

Despite its modest size; the name of Mucking is internationally famous as the site of a unique Migration Age Saxon settlement. Excavations on the site began in 1965 and continued for over a decade. Originally initiated because of cropmarks shown up in aerial photography, the excavations recovered a landscape palimpsest revealing layer upon layer of human settlement from the Mesolithic to the post-medieval periods. The excavated area lies on higher ground about 1 km west of Mucking church, and extends for about 1 km on a north-east/south-west orientation above the 20 m contour. There is a significant – for Essex – escarpment here, facing the Lower Hope and curving across the Thurrock peninsula where it produces fine views at points such as Gun Hill and Rookery Hill. The escarpment is in fact the 'Thames terrace', its gravel soil providing the first firm surface above the marshy areas below. It is this gravel which was partly the cause of recovery of the archaeological remains at Mucking; a valuable ingredient in the modern construction industry, the proposed stripping of the gravel at Mucking accelerated the need for total excavation before destruction.

It is difficult to summarize the discoveries of over a decade of archaeological work and a further decade of post-archaeological activity. However, this Mucking hillside revealed human activity commencing in the Mesolithic and Neolithic, with occasional finds of flints indicating migrants or hunters passing through the area. In the early Bronze Age the first settlement appeared, reflected in traces of agricultural activity. This was later followed by the construction of a 'mini hillfort', an 80 m wide circular earthwork with double-walled defence. In the Iron Age times seem to have been more peaceful, as the fortifications disappear to be replaced by a settlement of round houses. This developed, in the later Belgic period, into a complex pastoral settlement. Rectangular buildings were introduced and a network of field boundaries and enclosures established or improved. These have been interpreted as sheep folds; loomweights found also support this interpretation. Coins, brooches and wheel-thrown pots were also found. After the Roman conquest land use was intensified and the area was incorporated into a large-scale rectilinear field-system covering the whole of the Thurrock peninsula. A villa lay in the immediate vicinity; Roman tiles, wall daub and window glass have all been found on site. There were two Romano-British cemeteries.[204]

At the beginning of the fifth century Saxon occupation began on site; this comprised a large settlement with two associated cemeteries. Both cemeteries and settlement revealed much about the inhabitants. There were large quantities of pottery and domestic goods, and many beautiful high-status items of glass and metal. The settlement seems to have disappeared by the seventh century, perhaps partly by dispersal, and partly by moving to the more sheltered site of present-day Mucking.[205]

The Saxon settlement at Mucking was the first site where cropmarks of sunken huts have been proved by excavation and the first where extensive settlements *and* (two) cemeteries have been excavated. It incorporates the first large mixed cremation and inhumation cemetery to have been excavated in its entirety, and the first and only site where late Roman bronzes have been found both in Saxon graves and in Saxon huts. It also produced the largest assemblage of early fifth-century domestic pottery and an exceptional amount of fine metalwork.[206]

The excavated settlement consisted of more than 200 sunken huts or houses as well as fifty ground-level buildings, including several 'hall' type buildings. There were over a thousand graves in the two cemeteries, and many other features excavated such as wells, and ditches. The sunken house or *Grubenhaus* is a characteristic of early Saxon settlement; there were a number of different types and varying sizes, but all were constructed quickly and cheaply by digging out a layer of topsoil, stacking it alongside the dug-out area to form low walls, which were then roofed over with thatch, bracken or turves resting on rafters. The walls may have been faced on the inside with planks or logs, while the gable ends would also have been closed off with logs or planks.[207] There has been some debate as to whether *Grubenhauser* also had plank flooring so that the sunken area then became a kind of cellar. Some may have done so – and reconstructed examples can be seen at West Stow (see separate entry under Sites in Other Counties, Suffolk) – but at Mucking the rammed earth formed the floor level. There were advantages to such a building technique. It was quicker and cheaper to dig down, the maximum headroom being obtained for minimum effort, as well as greater protection against the weather. American settlers in the Great Plains used a similar building technique in the nineteenth century.[208]

Most of the buildings are aligned east–west, and of the ground-level buildings ('halls') excavated, most follow a similar plan, being double 6 m squares outlined by post-holes, with gaps for entrances on the long axis and an internal partition at the east end. This is paralleled in Continental sites such as Wijster and Flogeln,[209] as well as bringing to mind descriptions of halls from literature of the period.

The finest pieces found at Mucking are displayed in the British Museum (see entry under Sites in Other Counties, London). As well as a wide variety of pottery, both funerary and domestic, fine glass beakers were recovered and a fascinating range of metalwork. This included dress ornaments such as beads, pins and brooches as well as iron buckles, knives and shears, and bucket fittings. More important were the late Roman-style military bronze belt fittings; other military gear included swords and shield bosses. Some bone objects such as combs were also found, in spite of the soil's acidity. Clay loomweights, melted lead and iron slag suggest woollen and metalworking industries.

The significance of finding such a large and rich site as Mucking is clear, and its discovery and excavation attracted wide publicity, particularly the recovery of the 'sand-men', the body shadows still discernible in the earth even though soil acidity had destroyed all trace of the bodies themselves. Mucking has transformed our knowledge of early Saxons in Essex, and has enabled a re-interpretation of Saxon rural settlement in the county.[210]

What was the significance of the site itself? On land that was probably marginal even in late Roman times, but commanding a strategic view of London's sea approaches, a new and architecturally alien Saxon village sprung up. There seems to have been little continuity with the previous Roman landscape features; the villa nearby must have been abandoned in the very earliest phases of Saxon occupation if not before.[211] However, the presence of late Roman military belt fittings implies Roman or sub-Roman approval or direction for the settlement. Mucking is best seen as a military outpost, occupied by *foederati* or *laeti*, Roman-organized, treaty-controlled settlements of Germanic mercenaries and tribespeople. In this case, the site of the settlement seems to have been chosen to guard the approaches to London by detecting and monitoring shipping movements in the lower Thames.[212] Mucking's excavator, Margaret Jones, compared the site's sunken huts to the Nissen huts of the Second World War:

> low cost, easily erected shelters, useful for soldiers, refugees, immigrants, stores, camp followers, camp traders . . . a sort of transit camp for sudden influxes of homeless people, a first landfall after a North Sea crossing, with most of their wealth on their bodies, on their way to resume their farming role, and found anglicized Saxon villages in their new country.[213]

Location: As a result of large-scale gravel excavation in the area and total site excavation, nothing remains of the Saxon settlement at Mucking. The quarries in the area give this part of the Thurrock peninsula the appearance of a moonscape, and a large landfill site provides a social but definitely not a visual amenity. However, on a clear day a trip around the fringes of the site can give a good idea of the extent and function of Mucking's Saxon settlement. Start from the A13 junction with the A1014 for Stanford-le-Hope, and take the A1013. By train, alight at Stanford-le-Hope and turn left out of the station following London Road until it joins the A1013. Once on the A1013, after about 1/2 km, turn right into Buckingham Hill Road (signposted to Linford and East Tilbury). Pass the tip on your right and the quarry further along on the left. Suddenly, on the left, there is a view over the whole of what was the Mucking settlement; a plateau of grassland with pylons marching across it and delimiting the settlement boundary along the edge of the gravel terrace. Beyond lies the Thames, with some spectacular views downriver, reminding the observer of Mucking's original founction. Turn left into Walton's Hall Road. High hedges obscure the view at first, but then there is quite a good panorama to the left and upwards of the scarp which supported the settlement. An idea of its size can be gained too – it stretched almost to Butts Lane; this is the left fork at the junction with Mucking Wharf Lane and will return the visitor to London Road/A1013. There is no easy parking in the area and much industrial traffic.

Newham: see entry for Barking

Newport
Earliest known form of name: **Neuport**
Derivation: new town

Many people come to visit Newport to admire its fine vernacular buildings. There are houses dating from the fifteenth to the eighteenth centuries, and a delightful example of that Essex craft pargeting at Crown House. But on the edge of Newport stands a monument to an age far older.

The famous Newport Leper Stone, a great glacial boulder, tumbled to its present resting place in a far-off Ice Age, and has remained an object of awe ever since. It stands about $1\frac{1}{2}$ m high, and is as broad round as many a tree trunk. The stone stands beside the wall of Shortgrove Park, and set into this wall are a number of carved stones which help to explain the Leper Stone's curious name. These ornamental stones originally came from an old building known as Hospital Farm which stood in what is now Shortgrove Park and which was demolished towards the end of the last century.[214] Hospital Farm is traditionally supposed to have been the last remains of a leper hospital, set up by one Richard Serlo, in the reign of King John.

It was said that lepers from this hospital would place their orders for food etc. and the money to pay for it on this stone in the large hollow on top, which was usually full of water. The theory was that the water would cleanse the money from its leprous associations. The hospital was further granted the right to hold a fair to raise funds every St Leonard's day (6 November). St Leonard is the patron saint of prisoners and captives, but that may be irrelevant. The hospital was suppressed in the reign of Henry VIII. The only problem with this tale is that though there was a hospital, there was no evidence that it was ever a leper hospital. The county's founding historian, Morant, described the hospital in some detail but made no mention of lepers.[215]

However, the Leper Stone's story now has some interesting elements; taboos about approaching it, cleansing water held in a hollow, offerings of money. Such elements could well be remnants of the veneration of this stone. Prehistoric men were no doubt awestruck by this monolith; is it not likely that, as at Beauchamp Roding, this respect continued into Saxon times, and eventually became garbled, rationalized, and bowdlerized into tales of contamination by lepers, and the cleansing powers of its water? One writer has suggested,

> the real reason for the depressions [i.e. in the top of such stones] dates back to the time when stone worship was common. Even today, in some places, similar hollows are filled with flowers at certain times in the year, so at one time the Essex stones might have held sacrifices or, at least, thanks offerings.[216]

Location: Newport lies on the B1383 about 3 km south-west of Saffron Walden. The Leper Stone lies at the north end of Newport on the east side of the Cambridge Road, outside Shortgrove Park. Parking is difficult in the immediate vicinity. Newport has its own railway station.

Prittlewell
Earliest known form of name: **Pritteuuella** 1086 (DB)
Derivation: the babbling stream or spring

South-east Essex is now known to have been the scene of some of the earliest Germanic migration into the country. Sunken-floored huts typical of the earliest phase of settlement have been found at Barling[217] and at Temple Farm, Sutton,[218] and it has recently been confirmed that the pagan Saxon burial-ground near Priory Park at Prittlewell first came into existence in the sixth century. Some of the grave goods were distinctively Kentish, which may indicate small-scale settlement or trade from across the Thames.[219]

The view over the Blackwater Valley from Beeleigh Road, on the north side of the Maldon *burh*

The Newport Leper Stone, a possible focus for pagan veneration

Byrhtnoth, the hero of the epic Anglo-Saxon poem *The Battle of Maldon*

St Cedd, the Apostle of Essex

The seventh-century blocked Saxon door at Prittlewell church

The causeway to Northey Island, site of the Battle of Maldon AD 991

A deeply splayed window in the perfect Saxon church at Rivenhall

The Hangman's Stone from Littlebury, now forming part of a grotto in Saffron Walden, may well be a remnant of paganism. It can be seen to the right of centre with a hole bored in it

The magnificent gatehouse to the Priory of St Osyth – did this remarkable lady really carry her severed head from here to the parish church?

The Battle Ditches in Saffron Walden

Strethall church is a Saxon gem in the heart of Essex

The church at Sturmer, home of one of the Battle of Maldon heroes Leofsunu

A detail of Saxon long-and-short
work at Strethall

The Strood – a seventh-century causeway onto Mersea Island

The magnificent view from *Thunors leah*, the clearing dedicated to Thunor, now known as Thundersley

The lonely Thames-side marsh at Tilbury where St Cedd built his chapel of *Tilaburg*

A pillar dedicated to the god Thunor once stood on this barrow at Tolleshunt Major

The traditional tomb of Harold II, the last Saxon king of England, at Waltham Abbey

A blocked doorway at West Bergholt church. The church, in the Colne Valley, is a fine example of Saxon workmanship

Saxon long-and-short work can be seen at the corners of the walls of 'England's Oldest House' at Widdington

Nearby stands the church of St Mary the Virgin, Prittlewell, Southend-on-Sea's mother church. Its fifteenth-century pinnacled tower looks down on an important group of medieval buildings across the road. Local tradition makes this church a foundation of St Cedd,[220] and as if in confirmation the inner face of a Saxon door arch was revealed in the north wall of the chancel when a memorial slab was re-sited in 1931.[221] The arch was built from Roman bricks, and can be seen from both inside and outside the church. Opinions differ wildly about its date;[222] Ellis Gowing, the vicar at the time of the discovery, was convinced that the arch was part of a chapel built by St Cedd.[223] For once, local tradition seems to have been proved right: recent work has shown that the foundation plan of the church closely resembles the standard design of seventh-century monastic churches such as Bradwell-on-Sea,[224] built by St Cedd.

The Central Museum in Southend town centre houses many Saxon artefacts from south-east Essex. There is a case and a half together with an explanatory panel on the subject of the Saxons, together with smaller interpretative panels on 'The Saxon Hall', 'The Rise of Written English', and 'Building in Stone', together with descriptions of shipbuilding and a model of the Oseberg ship. There are reproductions of pottery from Mucking, and a panel on metalwork is displayed together with an early Anglo-Saxon knife from Prittlewell and a sword with scabbard fittings from the Anglo-Saxon cemetery at Prittlewell.

Panels on pagan burials, Saxon weapons, textiles, Saxon jewellery and the Anglo-Saxon penny are also complemented with relevant artefacts: two shield bosses from Prittlewell; a reconstruction of a bone comb *c.* AD 600 from Prittlewell; an early Saxon dolphin buckle from Shoebury; a fifth-century needlework set from Shoebury including a very dainty little pair of shears and two needles; a lead token *c.* AD 800 possibly used for the payment of customs duties; two *sceattas* from AD 700; a penny of Alfred and a penny of Cnut; some unprovenanced loomweights, and a head dressed in Anglo-Saxon fashion with appropriate jewellery.

Under the heading 'Rural Life' we find further material. There is a fifth-century bowl and an urn from North Shoebury. From Prittlewell comes a seventh-century hand-made bottle, and a glass vase, probably continental in origin. There is also a biconical bowl and two skulls from the same place. One of the skulls is mysteriously marked 'Female of Romano-British stock'. Also from Prittlewell and dated from the sixth century are two shearblades, an iron knife, as well as a seventh-century spearhead. There is a further, undated, spearhead from Westcliff.

Location: St Mary's, Prittlewell, stands in Victoria Avenue, about 1 km north of Southend-on-Sea's town centre. The nearest station is Southend Victoria, also in Victoria Avenue, and there are frequent buses from the railway station. Parking is difficult in the area. The church is normally kept locked; for access contact the vicar on 0702 43470.

Southend Central Museum stands adjacent to Victoria Station. The museum is open Monday, 10 a.m. to 1 p.m., Tuesday to Saturday, 10 a.m. to 5 p.m. Admission is free.

Rivenhall

Earliest known form of name: **Reuenhala** (1068)
Derivation: probably from (*aet þaem*) *hreofan heale*, 'at the rough nook'

Although nearly a third of all the medieval churches of Essex incorporate Roman brick in their fabric, only a select few are actually built over Roman buildings.[225] These include Alphamstone, Rivenshall, Stansted Mountfitchet and West Mersea. At Rivenhall, the church of St Mary and All Saints stand directly over a Roman villa.

The Rivenhall villa is an interesting example of its type. The main building consisted of three wings, together with a second, high-status building built on a podium. It is this second building which lies across the chancel of the present-day church. The relative splendour of the villa, its early date of construction (AD 70–80) and its proximity to Colchester and the Roman site of *Canonium*, Kelvedon, make it likely that this was the home of a British chieftain who supported Roman rule and who had adopted Roman ways.[226]

Later in the Roman occupation, a long, aisled barn was added to the west wing (that is, the wing nearest the present-day church), and in the fifth-century this barn seems to have been converted into an aisled hall to house Germanic folk. A fifth-century well and hearth were found in excavation, together with very early Anglo-Saxon pottery and glass. The implication is that Germanic people were brought in deliberately in the fifth century, perhaps to guard the villa owners during those turbulent times.[227] The aisled hall was abandoned in the sixth century, but a new hall extending from part of the villa was constructed, maintaining the continuity of the settlement.[228] Later, a chapel or mausoleum was built on top of the villa ruins, to be replaced in the tenth century with a small timber church, the plan of which was recovered during intensive archaeological investigation between 1971–8.[229]

Towards the end of the Saxon period, the present stone church was built. The great antiquity of this church, however, was masked by rendering over the fabric, and other modern additions; in his most spectacular error of dating, Pevsner was almost a thousand years out in dating the church from the early nineteenth century.[230] It was only when this disguise was removed in 1972 that the truth was realized. Now the visitor can see the courses of Roman brick and a Saxon window arch in the north wall of the chancel, with similar results being revealed as the south wall is also stripped. Stand at the eastern end of the graveyard and look out over the field beyond. There where the land dips and sheep now graze today, the Roman villa stood. Nothing is visible today in this pleasant sheltered spot, where the first generation of Anglo-Saxons stood guard over the last generation of Romano-Britons. Behind, the church stands testimony to the continuity of settlement in this well-watered valley.

Location: Rivenhall lies between Witham and Kelvedon, just off the A12. Follow signs for Silver End from the eastbound carriageway only. There is some parking on the verge outside the church. Although there are occasional summer Sunday openings, the church of St Mary and All Saints is normally kept locked; the key is kept at a nearby house; for location see the notice in the porch. The Saxon fabric can be seen from the outside, however.

Saffron Walden
Earliest known form of name: **Waledana** 1086 (DB)
Derivation: valley of the Britons

Saffron Walden is one of the county's prettiest towns. Visitors come to see the fine parish church, the local museum or the stump of the medieval castle which lies in its grounds. Its 'Saffron' title is medieval, given because of the local importance of its cultivation, but the 'Walden' element harks back to the period of the earliest Saxon settlement.

The Saxons called the area *weala-dunu*, the 'valley of the Britons'; the name suggests that here, at least, a distinct British community existed under agreement with its Saxon neighbours, in the fifth and possibly sixth centuries. What they themselves called their enclave is unknown, and archaeologists have still to identify the exact location of the post-Roman settlement. Nearby lies the pre-Roman hillfort of Ring Hill, at Littlebury, while a small Roman walled settlement existed near Great Chesterford a mile further north. Excavations prior to the site's destruction for gravel-digging before the Second World War revealed a rustic community of simply-built houses. No mosaics were found inside the walls, and the roads of the community were of the unplanned British style, so unlike the chess-board layouts of the big Roman cities.

A recent study[231] of parish and other boundaries in the area seems to have revealed the actual territorial extent of this sub-Roman state, which occupied a rough oval astride the Roman road now represented by the A11 at Great Chesterford, standing at the centre of the enclave, which also includes part of the Icknield Way. The circuit follows much of the eastern and southern parish boundary of Saffron Walden, then the southern boundary of Littlebury, across Elmdon and Chrishall and into Cambridgeshire. Once there the circuit swings round Duxford before turning back to Essex and following the county boundary at Great Chesterford, and so back to Saffron Walden. At the enclave's 'top end' the Roman road is cut by the Brent Ditch. This, like the better-known Devil's Ditch nearby, is an early Saxon defensive dyke cutting the Roman road. Its defences directly face the Walden statelet.

Saxon occupation, almost certainly peaceful and extending over a long period, did finally take place in Saffron Walden, where the earliest Saxon settlement lay around Abbey Lane; a cemetery was excavated here in the nineteenth century. The later graves were east–west orientated suggesting Christian burial, which was reinforced by the absence of grave goods, except for one female burial which contained a fine pendant and necklace decorated in the Viking style.

At the end of the Saxon period the growing town, which seems to have been largely to the west of the High Street,[232] was fortified with a defensive earthwork. This took the form of a ditch and bank, parts of which are still visible today. These earthworks were once thought to be no earlier than the thirteenth century, when they were known as the *magnum fossatum*. Archaeological investigation has, however, demonstrated their Saxon origin.[233] Known today as the Battle or Repell Ditches, they encircled the town with the possible exception of the marshy area to the north-west beside The Slade, now occupied by the sewage works.

The north–south axis of the ditch was the High Street. The earthwork enclosed the area now contained (very roughly, and using modern streets as reference points) in the following anti-clockwise circuit: from the southern end of the High Street, along Audley Road, left up Fairycroft Road, up Common Hill, Castle Hill and Catons Lane, then left, crossing Bridge End Gardens, over Bridge Street to the western end of the sewage works, then turning south across open land to cross Abbey Lane and meet the extant section south of it, turning left again along the embankment and back to the High Street along Margaret Way.

Most of the ditch has been occluded by urban development – including the castle bailey as far back as the twelfth century! The best extant section is, as already mentioned, on the left-hand side at the end of Abbey Lane, which runs off the High Street. An impressive ditch and bank can be followed for about 150 m before it turns east with a further 150 m stretch running into Margaret Way.

Now resting in great obscurity in the town is one of the most impressive pagan stones in Essex. It is a monumental standing stone or erratic of a type known as 'Hangman's Stones'. It stood originally in the adjacent parish of Littlebury, and the following tale is told of it.[234] One night a sheep stealer took a sheep. He tied its legs together, swung the rope over his head and set off for home. Feeling tired *en route* he rested his back and the sheep against a large stone. The sheep began to struggle and slipped over the far side of the stone, strangling the thief. Next morning the two were discovered, hanging on either side of the stone, a deep indentation running across the top of the stone caused by the rope's friction in the dying man's struggles. This story is known in half a dozen parts of the country, in varying versions, including Yorkshire.

In the nineteenth century the stone was removed from Littlebury by one Jabez Gibson and placed in his garden in Saffron Walden. At some stage, the stone became incorporated into a stone folly or summer-house. Gibson's house, then called Elm Grove, later Walden Grove, has been demolished, and in its place now stands sheltered housing for the elderly. The summer-house/folly still stands in the grounds, however, though in a very neglected and dilapidated condition. The Hangman's Stone, on the south side of the structure, is quite unmistakeable, being so much larger and darker than the other stones used.

Saffron Walden is fortunate to possess a superb local museum. Comfortably housed in a fine old building, the museum's imaginatively displayed ethnographic collection is of national if not international importance.

History is portrayed in the Ages of Man gallery, with a number of items from our period of interest. Here we can see the 'Daneskin' from the door of Hadstock church; the label speculates that the skin may have been that of a Dane caught during a raid and flayed to death. There is much excavated material from the Saxon settlement site at Bonhunt, including a reconstruction of a Saxon loom, together with weaving implements and other domestic goods such as rings, pins, combs and knives. A drawing shows a reconstruction of a middle Saxon aisled hall. A special display shows 'The Burial of a Nobleman', illustrated by the rich finds from a cremation burial not in Essex but from Combe in Kent. These include a spectacular sword with a decorated hilt, a bronze hanging belt, beads, brooch parts and textile fragments.

From the mainly Christian cemetery within the Battle Ditches come two Saxon burials, cleverly displayed – the two skeletons are sunk in a glass floor. Also from this cemetery and dating from the late ninth century are the grave goods of a pagan Viking lady; a necklace with ornamented silver-gilt pendants, beads of silver, cornelian, crystal and glass.

There are also two silver pennies of Alfred found at Ashdon, part of a hoard which included late ninth-century Viking and French coins. Part of a coin hoard from the River Ribble in Lancashire is also displayed, an early tenth-century hoard containing 7,000 coins in all, probably lost by Vikings fleeing from Dublin. An informative panel 'Walden History in Buildings' explains the history of pre-Norman Walden, developing the theme of continuity in the 'valley of the Britons'.

Location: Saffron Walden lies near the M11 and the B1383 (the old A11). From the M11 leave at junction 9 and take the B184. The nearest station is Audley End (4 km). All the sites mentioned are within a few minutes' walk of one another. The footpath along the ditches starts off in Abbey Lane. The Hangman's Stone is in the grounds of a private old people's home off Elm Grove, which lies off Fairycroft Road. The museum, which is open from Monday to Saturday 11 a.m. to 5 p.m. (April to September) or Monday to Saturday, 11 a.m. to 4 p.m. (October to March), stands off Museum Street, and there is ample parking in the museum grounds. There is a charge for admission.

Saint Osyth

Earliest known form of name: **Cicc** *c.* 1000
Derivation: meaning unknown. The village was not known as
St Osyth until at least 1187.

The bustling and picturesque village of St Osyth is situated at the
southern end of the Tendring peninsula. This part of Essex, more
than any other, shows the influence of Viking settlement. After the
Viking invasions of the late ninth century, there was considerable
settlement of Scandinavian peoples. This was concentrated in three
areas, each of which developed a separate administration under
Viking control; northern England (the kingdom of York), the
kingdom of East Anglia, and the Midlands (the Five Boroughs). Essex
lay to the east of the traditional dividing line (Watling Street) between
English and Danish law, and so came under Viking control. There is
little archaeological or historical evidence of their presence, however,
and as a frontier zone Essex was often a debatable land. Only in
Tendring do they seem to have settled in any numbers; this can be
inferred from place-name evidence, as this is the only part of Essex
where a cluster of Scandinavian place-names is to be found. These
occur at Thorpe-le-Soken, Kirby-le-Soken and Thorrington.[235] Other
place-names such as Frowick Hall in St Osyth (which may come from
Frothi's vik or creek), and Skighaugh in Great Oakley (possibly the
nook of Skeege) may incorporate Scandinavian personal names,
though some caution is required as many such names had Anglo-
Saxon equivalents. The name Harwich means army-dwelling, and it is
tempting to see this as a reference to a Viking camp set up there on
one of the many raids.[236]

   Turning now to the remarkable saint who gave her name to the
village, there are extraordinary legends of her life: traditionally,
St Osyth was the daughter of Frithuwold, who was known to have
been king of Surrey in 673,[237] and Wilburh, sister of King Wulfhere of
the Mercians. Hagiographies, or saints' lives, abound of early saints
and martyrs like St Osyth. Many elements of such hagiographies are
fantastical, stories of wonder and miracle for the credulous, or
perhaps, less cynically, they could be thought of as aids to devotion.
Many elements are traditional motifs from folk-tales with a pedigree
going back to time out of mind. Often, however, the stories have a
basis in fact, and although the earliest fragments of the *Vita* (saint's
life) of St Osyth are no older than the twelfth century, many of the
details of her family and early life are certainly plausible.[238]

She is said to have been born in Quarrendon in Buckinghamshire, and then brought up by her aunt, St Edith, at Aylesbury. Under the saintly influence of her aunt, Osyth was seemingly intent on becoming a nun, but her parents affianced her to Sigehere, king of the East Saxons. He ruled Essex jointly with his brother Saebbi from about 663–4. The date of his death is not known; it may have been in 683, or perhaps about 690. Sigehere is known to have abandoned Christianity after a plague in about 665,[239] though he was reconciled to the faith again after Wulfhere sent a bishop to him.

According to tradition,[240] Sigehere was passionately fond of hunting, and he chose the day of his wedding to Osyth to pursue a stray stag. This enabled the newly-married Osyth to flee to the safety of the East Anglian bishops Acca of Dunwich and Bedwin of Elmham, so that her vow of perpetual chastity could be ensured. Surprisingly, Sigehere seems to have acquiesced to the demands of his bride, and he allowed her to become a nun as she had always wanted. To help her, he granted her land at Cicc, on a creek between Brightlingsea and Clacton; here Osyth founded a monastery.

The monastery prospered for some time, but the east coast was said to be a dangerous place as there were frequent piratical raids. In one attack, marauders tried to abduct St Osyth. She resisted and the pirates cut off her head. As the Essex writer Bax noted,

> a genuine saint is often very little incommoded by a loss which would be grievous to lesser persons, and no right-minded reader will doubt the old monastic story that Osyth, taking up her head, walked to a neighbouring church where, body and head, she was buried.[241]

A spring is said to have gushed forth miraculously at the spot where Osyth was beheaded. The spring, Nun's Well, is still in existence in Nun's Wood on private land in the priory estate,[242] though it was still being shown with awe to visitors as recently as 1894.[243] It was said that the two raiders who beheaded her were the Danes Inguar and Hubba, but this is an anachronism as they were not active until two centuries later.

Osyth's body was moved to Aylesbury, supposedly because of the danger of further raids, but more probably because of a strong Mercian cult to her name. Many miraculous tales grew up about her life.[244] In one, relating to the time when she was under the care of St Edith, Osyth was blown off a bridge while crossing a river. After being submerged for three days, and being presumed drowned, she rose out of the water alive and well.[245] However, her body did not stay long at Aylesbury. After forty-six years it was moved back to Cicc, and re-interred in the monastery. Though little is known about the pre-Norman monastery at Cicc, the earliest reference to her cult there is from the early eleventh century, when the Register of Hyde Abbey notes that her body lay 'at Cicc near the sea in Saint Peter's mynster'.[246] In the official church calendars 7 October was marked as the day of her martyrdom.

The abbey was brought to new greatness in the twelfth century when it was re-founded, and a succession of splendid buildings erected down the centuries are still to be seen today in varying states of preservation. The abbey was dissolved in 1539, and its fabulous wealth dispersed. Chief among the relics was the skull of St Osyth encased in silver with a silver crown set upon its head; this had been in a shrine at the high altar. Soon after the Dissolution, the abbey passed to the D'Arcy family, and they made further alterations, as have successive owners down to the nineteenth century.

Nothing remains from the pre-Norman period at St Osyth Priory today. The earliest surviving parts of the building are the magnificent gatehouse, the chapel of St Osyth, the cellarer's range, and parts of the frater. The abbey church has vanished completely; it formerly lay about halfway between the gatehouse and the rest of the buildings to the north. Its high altar, displaying St Osyth's silver skull, would have stood approximately in the south-easternmost corner of the present-day topiary garden. In the thirteenth-century chapel there are reminders of Osyth's life and associations with the area, including a nineteenth-century stained glass window depicting Osyth and Sigehere.

St Osyth's Priory is a beautiful group of buildings in a unique setting. As the Essex topographer Bax wrote,

> To wander in the Park, within sight of the impressive old building, is to remember once more how rich and powerful the Church was at the time of the Dissolution, and how long is England's memory. Poor St Osyth would be surprised, no doubt, if she could know how her name persists; but, especially if the light of an evening in late summer is glowing upon the bricks and upon the woodland, it is difficult not to imagine how valiantly the young spirit of Christianity once battled here against the ignorance and ferocity of European paganism.[247]

Location: St Osyth lies on the B1027 between Colchester and Clacton-on-Sea (the nearest station). The priory lies on the western side of the village and is signposted. It is open to the public on Easter weekend and then from 1 May to 30 September daily; there is an admission charge. The church of St Osyth, Peter and Paul, where Osyth is said to have fallen dead and where she was first buried, stands opposite the priory across The Bury, and is normally kept locked; for access contact the vicar on 0255 820348.

South Benfleet

Earliest known form of name: **Beamfleot** *c.* 900 (ASC)
Derivation: tree-marked creek

In 1853–4 when South Benfleet station was being constructed, workmen turned up charred prows of ancient ships together with large numbers of human skeletons. This was dramatic confirmation of the *Anglo-Saxon Chronicle*'s account of the destruction of the Danish camp at Benfleet nearly a millennium before.

The end of the ninth century was one of the most turbulent periods of English history; for decade after decade Viking armies launched devastating attacks so furious and overwhelming that the English almost disappeared as a nation; only the superb military skill of King Alfred saved the day. From 865 onwards the Danes came as invaders rather than pillagers. By 879 Danes occupied half the country, from East Anglia to York. Essex was also occupied. The country was partitioned in 886 along a line following the River Lea and Watling Street. Beyond the Lea lay London and the still free lands of Wessex.

From 892 onwards, however, there was further violence when a fresh Danish army landed and began ravaging southern England. Part of this army, its leader named Haesten, crossed into Essex and set up camp at Benfleet after being defeated by Alfred's forces. Haesten was forced into a peace treaty and had Christian baptism imposed on his two sons. The rest of the army had raided westwards but by 893 were also forced to retreat to Benfleet. A very large and dangerous army was now camped at Benfleet, and the English assembled a militia from the London garrison and West Saxon reinforcements to attack it. Unwisely, Haesten left the fort for a raid into Mercia.

The *Anglo-Saxon Chronicle* records what happened:

With the citizens (of London) and the help which came to them from the west, they (the English forces) went east to Benfleet . . . Haesten had made that fort at Benfleet before this, and was then off on a plundering raid while the great host was in occupation.

Then the English advanced, and put that host to flight, stormed the fort, and seized everything inside it, both property and women and also children, and conveyed them all to London: and all the ships they either broke up and burned up or brought to London or to Rochester. And Haesten's wife and his two sons were brought to the king, and he restored them to Haesten because one of them was his godson and the other was the godson of earldorman Aethelred.[248]

Although the Danish fleet had been captured or destroyed, the host itself remained intact, to strike again from Shoebury (see entry for South Shoebury). But can any trace now be found of the Danish camp at South Benfleet? The discovery of the burnt boats at Benfleet station implies that this was the beach-head where the boats were drawn up, with the encampment further inland on higher ground. Most writers concur that the camp's site was likely to have been in the vicinity of the parish church of St Mary,[249] though at least one writer took the opposite view; that the camp was on the opposite bank of Benfleet Creek, on Canvey Island.[250]

St Mary's stands in the shade of some fine sycamores at the western end of a bluff of high ground above the creek, overlooking Benfleet Marsh. As long ago as 1903 the very steep slope on the western side of the churchyard was seen as remnants of a glacis or artificial scarp built as part of the Danish camp.[251] A commemorative plaque next to the lychgate reads: 'The Battle of Benfleet AD 894. The Danes occupied a fortified encampment situated hereabouts. Their army was defeated and driven out by the troops of King Alfred the Great'. A lane, St Mary's Close, leads us round to what is believed to have been the north-west corner of the camp; a stream flows down towards Benfleet Creek but it hardly seems large enough to have carved the very large gully we encounter. It may be a natural cleft which has been artificially widened.[252] At the bottom of the churchyard this 'fortification' peters out, though if it stretched to the creek it must have roughly followed the course of the High Street down to the station. How far it extended to the east is not known. The defences may have taken the form of a moated embankment, following the stream north, round the top end of the churchyard and extending back to the creek along an imagined continuation of High Road.

Location: St Mary's Church lies at the junction of Benfleet High Road and High Street. Benfleet Station lies about 100 m to the south, and there is a car-park in the station. The church is normally kept locked.

South Shoebury

Earliest known form of name: **Sceobyrig** 894 (ASC)
Derivation: fortification on the shoe-shaped piece of land

This is a corner of Essex bleak in winter and bracing in summer. The 'byrig' in the place-name refers to the great Danish camp built by Haesten after his fortress at Benfleet had been overrun by Alfred's men. The site, close to the sea, was built over by the Artillery Barracks in 1858 and has been all but obliterated in the years since. Street names in the area are virtually all that reminds us of invasion and battle; Rampart Street, Dane Street, Hinguar Street (after Ingvar, the Danish leader).

The tale of Shoebury Fort follows on directly from that of South Benfleet (see separate entry). After the destruction of the Benfleet camp in 893, Haesten and his formidable Danish army retreated to Shoebury, where he built a new camp. This was the base for a new raid the following year across to the Severn Valley, but they were defeated and fled back to Shoebury. A second raid took them to Chester and into Wales, but by 894 a scorched earth policy by the English forced them once more to retreat back into Essex, to a new temporary camp on Mersea Island (see separate entry on East Mersea). Shoebury camp seems to have been abandoned, for soon after arriving on Mersea the Danish force moved off again and set up a fresh camp on the River Lea. They were dislodged from here when Alfred had the river blocked up, and the force moved inland to Bridgnorth, where they finally dispersed in 896.

Although Shoebury camp was only occupied for a short period it was a formidable stronghold. There are differing accounts of the size of the ditch and ramparts but the defensive capacity is clear. The ditch is variously reported as having been 40 ft wide and 5ft 6in deep in 1885, 8 or 9 ft deep in 1898 and 25 ft wide in 1908. Accounts of the rampart's height varied from 7 to 8 ft in 1885 and 12 ft in 1898.[253] It seems unlikely that the fort described a full circle as implied in the *Victoria County History*;[254] even though there has been considerable coastal erosion, it seems more likely that the camp was, from the first, in the form of the shallow horseshoe which survives today. Even now, the ends of the rampart are 500 m apart and the defences some 200 m deep.

There are no longer any visible remains of Shoebury camp on public land. However, the line of the rampart can be followed for a short distance along Rampart Street from Shoebury East Beach. The rampart then crossed the present-day entrance into Horseshoe Barracks and curved south-west into Army land, eventually turning back towards the sea. Small sections of the embankment are preserved within the barracks, which is not open to the public.

Location: Shoebury lies at the end of the A13. Rampart Street is off Shoebury High Street, and there is a large car-park on Shoebury East Beach. Shoeburyness Station stands in Shoebury High Street; turn right out of the station and Rampart Street lies about 100 m on, at the junction with Smith Street.

Southend-on-Sea: see entry for Prittlewell

Steeple Bumpstead
Earliest known form of name: **Bumsteda** 1096 (DB)
Derivation: place where reeds grow. The 'steeple' prefix is first recorded in 1267

St Mary's is a charming church in a charming village, with a tower rather than the expected steeple. *Stepel*, however, means 'tower' in Anglo-Saxon, though it has been suggested that the name referred to some nearby fortification rather than the church itself.[255] Within the church on the chancel door is a replica of the magnificent eighth-century shrine-mount found at the church and now on display in the British Museum (see entry under Sites in Other Counties, London).

The original shrine-mount was discovered during the construction of a vault at the east end of the church; at first it adorned a chest in the vestry before being placed on the chancel door where the replica is situated. When attached to the chancel door it was 'kept polished, as though it were any old door-knob'.[256]

The piece, a cast hemispherical boss of copper alloy, gilt and niello, is 12.8 cm in diameter and 3.6 cm in height, flanged, and with an extraordinarily intricate design, in three concentric rings, with settings for gemstones (now lost).[257] The top of the boss is a collar which once must have held a very large gem such as a piece of amber or crystal. Four cast fish-like monsters (which are, in fact, lions) climb the sides of the boss, and each of the little panels is finely decorated. The flange has intricate whorls, the next ring interlocked beasts, and the top ring has an elaborate interlocked triple-spiral pattern. The whole piece must have been a most glorious sight when it was complete, its gilt and missing gems, and probably filigree as well, making it a blaze of colour and light.

Stylistically, the boss is of Irish manufacture; the quality is of the very highest, finer than any other shrine-mounts of similar design now surviving (most of which found their way to Norway). It is fascinating to speculate how such a superb piece could have ended up in Steeple Bumpstead. What was the nature of the shrine which it adorned, and how did it become forgotten – was it buried to escape the Puritan iconoclasms?

Location: Steeple Bumpstead stands on the B1054 near Haverill and the A604. The village is signposted from the A604. The church is normally kept open and there is some parking outside.

Stifford

Earliest known forms of name: **Estinfort/Stifort** 1086 (DB)
Derivation: path-ford

Stifford church stands on a long ridge of high ground overlooking a wide curve of the Thames. It has a flinty tower with an elegant shingled spire which must have been a considerable landmark before the A13 gouged a great swathe across the lower ground to the south. The village of North Stifford is – perhaps surprisingly – picturesque, with thatched cottages and two fine Georgian buildings, Coppid Hall and the Moat House, now a hotel. Because Stifford is long and narrow, like many Thames-side parishes, a variety of land-types is included, from the riverside at South Stifford, across the marshes, and including the ridge at North Stifford. The ford referred to in the name crosses the Mardyke, which runs to the north of the church from Laindon on its way to Purfleet. The fabric of the church – dedicated to St Mary – dates mainly from the thirteenth century and comprises a mix of material; there is much pudding-stone in the south wall. Our interest, however, lies on the north side, where the wall at the north-west corner of the nave is built over a massive blackened pudding-stone well over a metre across.

As at Magdalen Lever, the church must have been built deliberately over this pudding-stone as a mark of subordination and subjugation of what may have been an older form of worship.

Location: Stifford church lies off the huge A13 intersection with the A1012; this goes south to Grays. Instead take the local road signposted to Stifford, on the north side of the roundabout. The church lies on the High Road, and parking is difficult in the immediate area. The church is normally kept locked but the pudding-stone is on the exterior.

Strethall
Earliest known form of name: **Strathala** 1086 (DB)
Derivation: the nook by the Roman road

'The deepest Essex few explore/Where steepest thatch is sunk in flowers', wrote John Betjeman in his poem 'Essex' in 1954. If anywhere is deepest Essex, it must be this remote corner beyond the M11, and all the more worth the attention of the wayfarer in search of the soul of Essex. Here is the church of St Mary the Virgin, as Mee says, 'one of the oldest buildings in Essex, a perfect little piece of Saxon architecture'.[258] The churchyard was full of birdsong when we visited.

The nave of the church is pure Saxon, the chancel arch too. The tiny nave is only about 9 m long by 5 m broad. From the outside, the typical Saxon long-and-short quoins can be seen on the corners of the western end. The south doorway also has long-and-short work in its jambs, and the low and narrow chancel arch is also Saxon

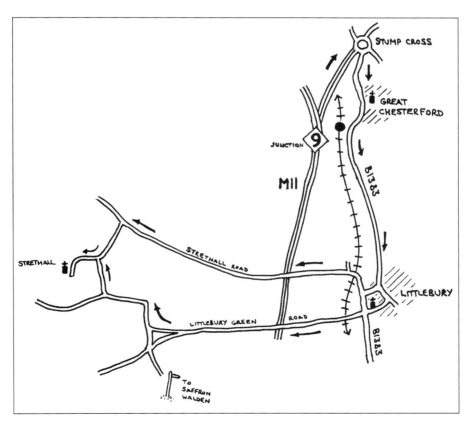

Strethall church

workmanship. The church guide asks the visitor to particularly note this arch, decorated with its three strips of different sections running up the sides and round the arch, as it is similar to one in a better-known Saxon church, that of St Benet's, Cambridge.[259] Pevsner decries these ornamental mouldings around the arch as 'illogical'[260] and meaningless, but Scarfe springs vigorously to the defence, noting that the 'mouldings mean Saxon work, and we rejoice in its survival, for its age and its design have given it a grace missing in much Norman work'.[261] Quite so. There are also two Saxon windows set very high in the western wall. The arched window can be seen fairly readily, but the small round window is higher still and can only be seen by peering up at the correct angle through the roof timbers.

Location: Strethall, as its name implies, stands on a Roman road, in this case the road between Braughing and Great Chesterford. However, although it is only a kilometre from the modern motorway, it is approachable only by minor roads, so much so that one guidebook urges that 'the approach is not to be recommended on a wet day, for the farm track is muddy and uneven'.[262] The best approach is via the B1383, between Great Chesterford and Bishop's Stortford. The B1383 is accessible from the M11 at junction 9 and the Stump Cross roundabout. From the B1383 turn off at Littlebury onto the Strethall Road (signposted), or the Littlebury Green Road. On the Strethall Road turn left after about 2½ km and right where the lane forks. On the Littlebury Green Road follow the right fork which appears after about 2 km, then turn right again. The road then twists left and into the hamlet of Catmere End, then right, then first left. The nearest stations are also on the B1383, at Audley End or Great Chesterford. The church is normally kept open.

Sturmer
Earliest known form of name: **Sturmere** (tenth century)
Derivation: the mere where the Stour arises

Sturmer is one of the most northerly parishes in Essex, and though it is not the Stour's source as its name implies, it does lie at the point where the Stour, winding down through Suffolk, first becomes the Essex boundary.

Here the nave of the little church of St Mary dates from the mid-eleventh century. It stands away from the village and next to Sturmer Hall, a fine moated medieval building refaced in brick, and hidden beyond a screen of trees. A gravel drive leads to the church, which is surrounded by a very well-tended churchyard.

The nave is built of coursed rubble. There is a blocked eleventh-century doorway in the north wall which has a rather unusual appearance. The windows are of the fifteenth century, but immediately east of the south wall's eastern window there are a few dressed stones which are probably part of a now-vanished eleventh-century window. The interior is plain and whitewashed; from inside, the most striking feature is the south wall of the nave, which is leaning outwards very alarmingly!

Sturmer was the home of one of the heroes of the Battle of Maldon in 991 (see entry for Maldon). Leofsunu bravely preferred death rather than flight when his leader Byrhtnoth was hewn down by the Vikings at that fateful encounter. As stated in the epic Saxon poem *The Battle of Maldon*:

Leofsunu spoke, raising his linden-shield aloft . . . 'I promise this, that I will not flee from this spot, but rather I will press on to avenge my lord . . . The steadfast men of Sturmer will not have cause to blame me; although my leader is dead I won't give up the fight. Let spear-point and sword-blade take me instead!'

In 1991, the Battle of Maldon Millennium Year, a handsome plaque was placed in the nave to commemorate Leofsunu.

Location: Sturmer lies on the A604 about 2 km east of the Suffolk town of Haverhill (which, incidentally, used to lie mainly in Essex until the nineteenth century, but that is another story). The church lies down the gravelled Church Walk at the western end of the village, and there is a grassed car-parking area adjacent to the church. When the gate giving access to Church Walk is locked, the nearest parking is in the nursery car-park. The church is normally shut; for access see the porch notice giving keyholders' addresses.

Thundersley
Earliest known form of name: **Thunresleam** (DB)
Derivation: clearing dedicated to Thunor

If anyone believes that Essex is flat, let them go to Thundersley and look out from the churchyard upon the wide view over the Crouch Valley and across to Basildon and beyond. For the Essex wayfarer, the county is full of sudden vistas and vantage points, not perhaps as spectacular as those that 'shire folk' may boast of, but satisfying to the traveller's eye nonetheless.

Thundersley takes its name from the god Thunor; here a clearing was dedicated to him. St Peter's Church may stand on the site of this clearing, commanding an inspiring view from the western end of a tongue of high ground. The stepped ranks of gravestones in the churchyard seem almost to tumble down the steep slope to New Thundersley below. The church has a shingled belfry and spire and a seven-hundred-year-old nave, now conjoined to a striking eastern extension built in the 1970s.

Location: Thundersley, often referred to as a 'dormitory town', lies sandwiched between the A13 and the A127, north of South Benfleet and south of Rayleigh (the nearest railway stations). The parish church of St Peter lies in Church Road off the A129 between Rayleigh and Benfleet. Halfway down the A129 is Hart Road. Follow this westbound until it becomes Church Road. The church lies on the left-hand side. There is a large car-park at the bottom of the hill, and a smaller parking area up the slope beside the church itself. The church is kept locked, but the view is freely available to all!

Thurstable

Earliest known forms of name: **Thur(e)stapel(l)**, **-stapl(e)** 1066–87
Derivation: *þunres stapol*, pillar of the god Thunor

Two hundred metres south-west of Tolleshunt Major's parish church, a tumulus stands sentinel in a field. This seems to have been the spot where 'Thunor's Pillar' was set up to mark the centre of the hundred (which later took the name of the pillar) and the meeting-place for the men of the hundred.[263] The place-name is one of a small group in Essex referring to the pagan god Thunor or Thor. Others are known at Thundersley ('Thunor's clearing'); Thunderley, in Wimbish, with the same derivation; and *Thunreslau* or Thunderlow, a now-lost place-name, but once the name of a half-hundred in north Essex in the Bulmer area, and meaning 'Thunor's Hill'.

The tumulus at Tolleshunt Major, which is circular with an indication of a ditch at the base, is about 2.5 m high and about 15 m wide; it has never been excavated. The rarity of pagan place-names in Essex indicates that paganism was in fact *common* and unremarkable, at least in the early days of the kingdom.[264] Tolleshunt Major lies at the centre of the Thurstable Hundred, which was a compact hundred bounded by the rivers Colne and Blackwater. It has been suggested[265] that the Thurstable area, together with an area covered by the later hundreds of Hinckford, Lexden, Tendring, Winstree and Witham, formed a discrete and resolutely pagan sub-kingdom within the kingdom of Essex, ruled by one of the branches of the royal house. According to that theory, St Cedd's choice of Bradwell-on-Sea, just across the Blackwater Estuary, as the starting point for his mission would thus have been aimed at converting this area of north-east Essex first.

The name Tolleshunt itself is curious in its own right. It is one of a group of very rare Anglo-Saxon place-names that incorporates a Latin loan-word. In this case, the loan-word is *fontana* ('spring'). The first element is the personal name *Toll*. Tolleshunt is the only example of the use of this Latin word in Essex, with the possible exception of Wicken Bonhunt (see separate entry). As the Saxons had their own perfectly good word for spring (*wella*), the implication is that place-names incorporating *fontana* meant something else, most likely some kind of stone trough, channel or other structure put up by the Romans to make the spring easier to use. All the places with the name-element *fontana* are associated with Roman remains nearby. That the Saxons adopted this word directly into Old English need not, however, imply contact between Saxons and Romano-Britons; they could just as easily have acquired the word on the European mainland.[266]

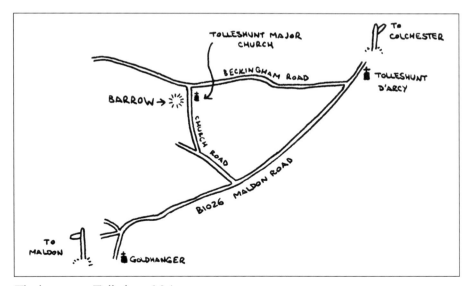

The barrow at Tolleshunt Major

Location: The Tolleshunt Major tumulus is situated off a minor road between Great Totham and Tolleshunt D'Arcy. D'Arcy can be reached either on the B1026 from Maldon or Colchester, or the B1023 from Kelvedon. At D'Arcy follow Church Street southbound out of the village, past the church and take the Beckingham Road to the right. Tolleshunt Major church lies about 2 km down this road, beside the moated Beckingham Hall on a minor road (Church Road) to the left. The tumulus lies in a field opposite the church. The field is *private property* but the tumulus can be adequately seen from the roadside, where there is plenty of parking space.

Waltham Abbey
Earliest known form of name: **Waltham** (1062)
Derivation: forest-homestead or enclosure

Waltham Abbey, or more correctly Waltham Holy Cross, is one of the few Essex towns of which an origin-legend has been preserved. Although some of the details may be obscure and puzzling, we are fortunate that the 'Legend of the Miraculous Cross of Waltham' has survived as a twelfth-century version of the town's foundation. The account, *De Inventione Sancte Crucis Nostre*, was written by a Canon of Waltham Abbey in about 1170; it has recently been paraphrased into English,[267] and subjected to thorough scrutiny.[268] This has shown that other relevant documents of the period support, if only circumstantially, many of the relevant details in the legend.

The tale begins in about the year 1030, not in Waltham Abbey but at Montacute (then known as Lutegaresbury) in Somerset, where a blacksmith had a series of compelling dreams in which he was ordered to dig for a buried cross on top of a nearby hill. After discussing the dreams with the parish priest, the blacksmith, priest and villagers went to the hilltop where, after digging, they discovered a carved black flint cross of Christ on the Cross, together with a smaller crucifix, a bell and a Bible, all under a big stone slab. The lord of Montacute at that time was Tovi the Proud, one of King Cnut's most important lieutenants. Tovi had the finds, with the exception of the smaller crucifix, put in a wagon drawn by twelve red oxen and twelve white cows, and a sign was sought to indicate where the finds should be taken. The wagon, however, resolutely refused to move until the name of Waltham was mentioned. This was where there was 'a little building [Tovi] had started to erect in the forest . . .

near to London, in a richly wooded spot with fertile pastures on the banks of the fishful River Lee'.[269] Various miracles occurred *en route* drawing a crowd of followers, of which sixty-six stayed with the Cross at Waltham and helped to found the monastery there.

Harold Godwinson, himself supposedly cured miraculously of paralysis at Waltham as a child, was later an important benefactor of the monastery, which he re-founded and to which he donated much land, as well as spectacular internal fittings. At the re-dedication ceremony, attended by Edward the Confessor, there was feasting for eight days and 'even vessels of wine and mead set out at the crossroads for the benefit of travellers'![270] Waltham became one of the most important shrines in the country, and in 1066 Harold, returning from the Battle of Stamford Bridge, stopped at Waltham Abbey on the way to Hastings. As he prayed before the Cross, the figure of Christ miraculously changed from looking upwards to looking downwards; this was interpreted as a bad omen. At the Battle of Hastings itself, the rallying cry of Harold's men was 'Holy Cross!'

After the battle, two Waltham brethren persuaded William to allow Harold's corpse to be interred at Waltham rather than at the intended Battle Abbey. They were unable to recognize his body on the field of battle, however, and Harold's mistress Edith Swanneck had to be called in to find the corpse. The body was buried with great pomp at Walthm at the eastern end of the abbey. At that time the abbey extended about twice as far as it does now, and had an apsidal end. The supposed site of his tomb is marked by a modern slab inscribed with 'Harold King of England Obiit 1066'. Before the Dissolution, the inscription read simply 'Harold Infelix' – Harold the Unlucky.[271] The Holy Cross disappeared at the Dissolution; its fate is unknown.

The church was doubled in size (making it nearly four times the size of the present church, and one of the largest in the country) in 1177 when it was re-founded by Henry II as penance for his murder of Thomas à Becket. In 1184 it became a 'mitred abbey', gaining immense power and prestige. It was the last abbey of all to be dissolved, in 1540, after which it was largely demolished. What remains is the seven-bayed Norman nave of great simplicity and strength, 'the noblest Norman nave in the south of England';[272] such is its reputation that in 1907, Waltham Abbey was a serious contender for the position of cathedral of the new Essex diocese.

Today the abbey ruins stretch away around the grave of the last Anglo-Saxon king of England. There is little today that he would recognize of the church he knew, though the east (external) wall of the Lady Chapel, once the transept wall of the larger church, is laid in herringbone fashion and believed to be Saxon workmanship. Excavations have uncovered several phases of the pre-Conquest church to the east of the present building, including Tovi's church, which had a rectangular chancel, and Harold's church, which had a transept and small apse.[273] An effigy of Harold stands in one of the niches outside the church, which is still dedicated to St Lawrence and Holy Cross. Inside the church there are three steps at the bottom right-hand corner of a window which can be seen high up above the further end of the aisle from the entrance to the Lady Chapel. The steps are completely worn out, though unused for 400 years, and so are thought to have been part of the pilgrims' steps which once led from the main body of the church to the shrine of the Holy Cross.[274]

Harold's tomb is the subject of a small pilgrimage on the Sunday nearest to 14 October by the *Engliscan Gesithas*, a group of enthusiasts for all things Anglo-Saxon. The so-called Harold's Bridge in the Lee Valley Park north of the town bypass dates from the fourteenth century. Today the few monastic remains have been laid out in pleasant gardens as part of the park.

Archaeological work in the abbey grounds has continued for some years, and the discovery and excavation in 1969–71 of a Viking-age hall seemed to confirm the legend's account of Tovi's 'little building' or hunting lodge at Waltham Abbey. About 30 m north of the church a hall 7.5 m wide and over 15 m long was discovered. The aisled hall had timbered gable ends and seems to have been turf-walled, with a single doorway at the western end. Evidence was also found for internal partitions and benches along the walls. Architecturally the hall differs from the distinctive Saxon aisled halls; the hall at Waltham had no post-holes indicating wall-posts (because the walls were free-standing turves) and was much narrower than similar Saxon aisled halls. The best parallel is with Viking-age buildings in Scandinavia, and given the evidence of the legend, it seems plausible that this was indeed the hall of Tovi, who no doubt arrived in England with Cnut as part of his retinue, and dates from the early eleventh century.[275]

Place-names and archaeological evidence indicates that Tovi's hall cannot, however, have been the first settlement at Waltham. Early, middle and late Saxon pottery has been found in the area of the later monastic precinct and market place – this was probably the extent of this earlier settlement,[276] and in character it may have been a royal estate dating from the settlement period AD 500–50. A study of the occurrence of the place-name *wealdham* (from which Waltham is derived) has shown that, like the place-name *wicham*, it is always associated with Roman roads and early Anglo-Saxon settlement, and additionally with wooded areas. There are twelve *wealdham* place-names in England, including three in Essex; these are Waltham Holy Cross, Great Waltham and Little Waltham. Most *wealdham* locations seem to have royal or high-status associations, and several gave their names to hundreds or sokes, indicating their importance. In such a context, therefore, *wealdham* seems to have meant 'royal estate from which a forest is administered' – this is an excellent description of Waltham Holy Cross. Topographical study has indicated that Waltham was the focus of a Saxon minster parish, its boundaries, which were themselves ancient landscapes divisions possibly dating back to the Iron Age, spanning the Lea. The Lea did not become a frontier until the Mercian occupation.

The church crypt houses an exhibition about the history of the abbey and town, and the Lee Valley Park Countryside Centre in Abbey Gardens has an exhibition about the history and natural history of the area. At the far end of Sun Street, the excellent Epping Forest District Museum houses displays relating to the whole of the Epping Forest District. Of relevance to the pre-Norman Waltham Abbey is pottery from various parts of the town, a Saxon skeleton from the town's seventh- to ninth-century cemetery, and various small finds from the Viking hall site. There is also, of course, much material from the abbey itself, but this is chiefly post-Norman.

Location: Waltham Abbey lies on the M25 and at the northern end of the A112, which follows the Lea Valley through Metropolitan Essex. From the north it is approached on the B194 which leads from Harlow. The town centre is well signposted from the M25 exit (junction 27). The nearest station is Waltham Cross, about 1 km across the Lea in Hertfordshire – this lies on the Liverpool St.–Cambridge line. The abbey church is normally kept open; the crypt centre is open 10 a.m. to 4 p.m. daily (except Sunday, 12 p.m. to 4 p.m. and Wednesday, 11 a.m. to 4 p.m.); during summer the centre remains open until 6 p.m.

The Lee Valley Countryside Centre is open daily from Easter to 30 September, from 10 a.m. to 5 p.m. Phone 0992 713838 for winter opening times. The Epping Forest District Museum is open Friday to Monday, 2 p.m. to 5 p.m., Tuesday, 12 p.m. to 5 p.m. Admission is free.

Wendens Ambo
Earliest known form of name: **Wendena** 1086 (DB)
Derivation: winding valley

The suffix *Ambo* is simply the Lation word for 'both', and was added to the name when the two parishes of Great and Little Wenden were united in 1662.[277]

The approach to the parish church of St Mary the Virgin is very picturesque, with a row of old Essex cottages and their English country gardens. The church has a Norman tower and nave. The chancel was rebuilt in the thirteenth century, when the south aisle was added. The north aisle was added a century later. It is the tower, with its little shingle spire (known as a 'Hertfordshire spike') which brings us to this corner of Essex, for it offers a fascinating lesson in the stylistic transition of architecture.

The core of the present church, which may have replaced an earlier building,[278] dates from the earliest years of the Norman Conquest.[279] But when the local craftsmen raised the tower at Wendens Ambo, they built it in the Saxon style which they knew best.[280] As a consequence, the Norman doorway is framed with a striking arch of Roman brick. A small window above is also arched with Roman brick. High up at the level of the belfry, round openings – two on the south and west faces, three on the north – called sound holes help to disperse the sound of the bells. These sound holes are a peculiarity of Saxon construction, and can also be seen on the tower of the tenth-century St Benet's Church in Cambridge.

Inside the church is an unexpected delight. A showcase displays an elegant piece of late Saxon pottery, which must be one of the few Anglo-Saxon artefacts on public display outside a museum. This brick-red crockern dates from the tenth or eleventh century and is of the type known as St Neot's ware. It was found during building work for the bungalow – now named St Neot's – together with other evidence of Saxon occupation about 200 m east-north-east of the old vicarage.

Location: Wendens Ambo lies on the B1039 about 3 km south-west of Saffron Walden. There is some parking in the lane leading to the church. By rail, Audley End is the local station, about 500 m from the church. The church is normally kept open.

West Bergholt
Earliest known form of name: **Bercolt** 1086
Derivation: hill wood

Here the redundant church of St Mary stands in the shadow of a great oak, beside West Bergholt Hall, a fine Georgian seven-bayed house. This is an ancient site – a prehistoric earthwork partly surrounds the churchyard.[281] In its secluded setting the church attracted little attention and was usually dated to the fourteenth century. After being declared redundant in 1975, however, a thorough investigation of the fabric was carried out by Robin Turner of Essex County Council.[282] When the external rendering was stripped away a late Saxon church was revealed beneath. The remains of a tall Saxon arched doorway can be seen in the north wall, and in the bell tower there are Saxon timbers re-used from an original Saxon bell-cage. Excavations revealed that the original church consisted of a nave and apsidal chancel; this goes some way towards proving that stone Saxon churches are more common than was once thought, and shows that the removal of rendering can reveal surprising results (see entry for Rivenhall).

Location: West Bergholt church is situated west of the village, off the B1508. Turn into Hall Road – there is a signpost to guide you to the church – and then into Old Church Road. The church lies about 1/2 km further on at the end of the road, and is normally kept open.

West Mersea
Earliest form of name: **Meres ig(e)** (ASC)
Derivation: island of the pool

Mersea Island is the heart of 'Mehalah Country', so named from Sabine Baring-Gould's powerful novel published in 1880 portraying the Mersea area as a wilderness of saltings, dark secrets, brooding and explosive passion.

The only road onto Mersea Island crosses the ancient causeway known as The Strood. The elegant summary of the island's topography written by historian Thomas Wright in 1836 still holds good:

The island is inaccessible from the land side except by a causeway called the Strode, which crosses the Pyefleet creek, and is covered by the sea at high water. The island is well-wooded and beautifully diversified with hill and dale; it has a bold commanding coast towards the German ocean, but on the north-west and south is low and flat, with a great extent of salt marshes.[283]

Because of the extensive Roman remains on the island, it had long been assumed that the origins of the Strood were Roman. However, work undertaken in 1978–80 conclusively proved that the causeway was Anglo-Saxon, dating from between AD 684 and 702.[284]

In 1978 contractors preparing a trench on the Strood for a water main discovered substantial oak piles underlying the earlier roadway levels. These were then dated both by dendrochronology (tree ring analysis) and radiocarbon dating, and both methods confirmed a late seventh-century date. No other causeway from this period is known in Britain. It has been estimated that between three and five thousand oak piles were used in the building of the causeway, which would have been a major project at that time, implying a central authority. It is likely that St Peter's Church at West Mersea was in existence and operating as a minster church at this period, so the causeway may have been built to enable the priests to get to the mainland dryshod. The king of the East Saxons at this period was Saebbi, who adopted a monastic lifestyle. Bede wrote of him, 'He devoted himself to religious exercises, frequent prayer, and acts of mercy, and he preferred a retired, monastic life to all the riches and honours of a kingdom'.[285] It is therefore not impossible that Saebbi himself used the Mersea minster as a retreat, ordering the causeway to be built to simplify his journey to the island.

Today the church of St Peter dates largely from the fourteenth century, but the main part of the tower is pre-Conquest. The church and nearby hall are built over a Roman villa; many mosaic pavements were found here in 1720 – Morant wrote an intricately detailed report of their discovery in his monumental history of Essex. The church's foundation is traditionally claimed to date back to Cedd himself.[286] Much of the church is built of re-used Roman brick and rubble, and in the tower some of the brick coursing is set in herringbone fashion.

Near the vestry door, on the south wall, there is a piece of carved Saxon stone about 450 mm x 150 mm. The stone has an interlace pattern sculpted on it, and the brass plaque set in the wall notes that it was probably a structural detail from the earlier church.

Location: Mersea Island lies at the end of the B1025. The church lies at the southern end of the High Street, and there is some parking in front of the churchyard. A local history museum stands nearby.

West Thurrock

Earliest known forms of name: **Tur(r)oc, Turocha(m), Thurrucca, Turrucca** 1086 (DB)
Derivation: from *thurroc*, the bilge of a ship

As the distinguished etymologist Margaret Gelling notes, this place-name is very appropriate for a stretch of marsh.[287] Set by the River Thames in marshland, this must always have been a remote spot. In some ways it is now more isolated than ever. There are no houses anywhere nearby, and a great industrial estate has grown up and now surrounds the church. The little tower of St Clement's, with its alternate flint and stone courses, is dwarfed by the huge Proctor and Gamble factory and the nearby power station. The appropriate dedication to St Clement is shared with that other Thames-side church, Leigh-on-Sea; St Clement was martyred by being thrown into the sea tied to an anchor, which became his symbol. The church, a scheduled ancient monument, is now redundant and its churchyard a wildlife conservation area.

The original church had a very different shape from the one which we see today, however. When first built in late Saxon (or perhaps very early Norman) times, the church had a round nave, like that at Little Maplestead. A chancel was attached, giving the building a 'key-hole' plan.[288] Apart from Little Maplestead, there are only four other surviving medieval round churches in the country, at Cambridge, Ludlow, Northampton, and the Temple in London.[289] The tower was built over the round nave in the fifteenth century. Apparently modelled on the Holy Sepulchre at Jerusalem,[290] very few other Saxon round churches are known to have existed. The church at West Thurrock is the smallest of them, the nave only 6 m in diameter. None of the others now survive.

First discovered as long ago as 1906,[291] the recent renovation of the church and churchyard was an opportunity to expose and conserve the foundations of the round nave, and these can now be seen around the base of the later tower. The investigation also served to indicate that the round nave was much more likely to be early Norman rather than late Saxon, so this site is only included for the sake of completeness. It is a fascinating spot nevertheless.

Location: St Clement's lies off the A126 between Purfleet and Grays. The nearest stations are at those towns, about 4 km and 3 km distant respectively. By car, turn off the A126 at the roundabout at the junction of West Thurrock Way and London Road – the church is signposted (as an ancient monument). Turn left out of Stone Ness Road into Hedley Avenue, then right into St Clement's Road. There is no vehicular access for the final 100 m, but plenty of parking space. The church is normally kept locked, but all the visible remains of the round nave are outside.

West Tilbury: see entry for East Tilbury

Wethersfield
Earliest known form of name: **Witheresfelda** 1086 (DB)
Derivation: probably *Wihthere*'s open country

Wethersfield is a hilly village in the upper valley of the Blackwater and, as several observers have remarked, it has much of the charm of its near neighbour Finchingfield yet none of the crowds. The parish church is dedicated to St Mary Magdalene and St Mary the Virgin; it has rather a strange-looking squat tower, topped with a wooden lantern and a copper-covered spire, giving it a Germanic appearance. As to the fabric of the church, much of its work dates from the thirteenth and fourteenth centuries, but the keen enthusiast can find fragmentary indications of the work of Saxon hands. At the western end of the north wall of the nave, where it joins the tower, masonry projecting from the arcade shows where an earlier stone church once stood before the Conquest.[292]

It has also been suggested[293] that the ancient belfry timbers have been re-used from an earlier building, perhaps the Saxon church, so these too may be pre-Norman.

Location: Wethersfield lies on the B1053 between Braintree (nearest station) and Saffron Walden. The church lies on the southern side of the village green, and is normally kept open.

White Notley
Earliest known form of name: **Hnutlea** 998
Derivation: nut-tree woodland

The Norman church of White Notley is one of a score of Essex churches whose dedication is unknown. It is a pretty church in a well-wooded setting; the little shingle spire tops a weatherboarded belfry, very characteristic of Essex. A little gem is concealed at the other end of the church. A modern vestry has been built onto the north wall of the chancel, but reset into the vestry's east wall is a tiny stone window which originally stood in the chancel. This window contains a rare piece of thirteenth-century glass with a crowned saint holding a book against a background of yellow irises. The round-headed window is, however, older still. The Norman architects who built the church re-used and re-shaped this stone from a Saxon headstone (architectural headstone that is, not a gravestone); part of the original Saxon masonry cuts can be seen on the exterior.

In the neighbouring parish of Faulkbourne, the church of St German's was long associated with a 'holy well', a Christianized relic of pagan water-spirit worship which probably stretches back even beyond Saxon times into the prehistoric period. There is or was a similar 'holy well' at St Peter's, Coggeshall, about 8 km to the north-east.[294]

Location: White Notley lies between Witham and Braintree, and has its own railway station on the Braintree branch line. By car it is probably best approached from the B1018 Braintree–Witham road, turning off at the signposted lane. There is no parking outside the church, but there is a large parking area across the road and slightly to the south. The church is normally kept locked; for access contact the rector on 0245 33256.

Widdington
Earliest known form of name: **Widintuna** 1086 (DB)
Derivation: willow farm

In the north-west Essex village of Widdington stands the only known Saxon building in the county in use as a private residence. Priors Hall, formerly known as Stone Hall, was thought until 1988 to date from the thirteenth century. However, it has now been established that a substantial part of it is a Saxon stone building,[295] earning Priors Hall the title of 'England's Oldest House'.[296]

The eastern end of the present house was once the western end of a double-celled building, each cell being 11.5 m long by 6.4 m wide. The walls, which are of mortared flint, seem to be more or less the Saxon walls surviving intact. At the north-east corner, when the rendering was stripped off, the tell-tale Saxon long-and-short quoins were revealed. Further examination of the eastern wall revealed a blocked doorway and windows. The doorway had long-and-short jambs and irregular voussoirs (the wedge-shaped stones forming the arch), and the window was possibly double splayed. These stylistic features all indicate a Saxon date. On the eastern end of the building, the stubs of the walls which originally formed the eastern cell of the building are still extant. Excavation further to the east exposed a robber trench (a trench once containing stone foundations, robbed at some point for re-use) on the same alignment, where the wall foundations of the eastern cell had once stood.

This double-celled building was probably a church or chapel, perhaps the manorial chapel. This particular manor belonged before the Conquest to Thorkell, and afterwards it was granted to the Abbey of St Valery in Picardy.

Location: Widdington lies on a minor road off the B1383 between Stansted Mountfitchet and Newport (nearest station, 4 km). Priors Hall is a *private house*, though some of the details of the Saxon architecture mentioned above can be seen from the nearby Priors Hall Barn. This is a fine medieval barn in an excellent state of preservation and now in the care of English Heritage. It contains some agricultural exhibits. The barn is open 1 April to 30 September at weekends and bank holidays only, and there is a small admission charge. Travelling south from Newport on the B1383 (London Road), take the signposted left turn to Widdington, and Priors Hall Barn is signposted on the right just before you enter the High Street of the village proper.

Witham
Earliest known form of name: **Wit ham** (913)
Derivation: unknown, though it may mean enclosure on a bend (in the River Brain)

Witham does indeed occupy a strategic bend in the Brain, shortly before it merges with the Blackwater. This spot was chosen for a fortified site as long ago as the Bronze Age, and Edward the Elder re-occupied it in 912 and built a *burh* there as part of his campaign to conquer the 'Danelaw'. This campaign was a protracted process lasting a quarter of a century. It consisted of three phases of consolidation, interspersed with sudden raids from both sides. Initially, the Wessex and Mercian heartlands were provided with fortified *burhs* so that the land could never again be entirely overrun in a surprise attack. Then the frontier areas were fortified with *burhs*, and finally, the frontiers were pushed forward and further *burhs* built to retain a hold on the captured territory. The Witham *burh* falls into this final category, and formed part of an advance into East Anglia, Essex and the South Midlands.

The *Anglo-Saxon Chronicle* notes the construction of the *burh* under the year 912 in characteristically laconic terms:

> In this year, about Martinmas, king Edward had the more northerly fortress at Herford built . . . Then afterwards, the summer after, between Rogation days and midsummer, king Edward went with part of his forces to Maldon in Essex, and encamped there whilst the earthwork at Witham was being built and stockaded: and a good number of people who had earlier been under Danish domination submitted to him.[297]

The *burh* has had an unfortunate history subsequently. Its original settlement, known as Chipping Hill, was eclipsed in 1212 when a new town, *Wulvesford*, was created beside the Roman road a short distance away, which then became the focus for settlement. And in the 1840s the Colchester railway cut straight through the middle of the fort, obliterating most of it. Housing development has continued from then to the present day, and has done yet more to obscure the site. However, enough remained of the site in the late nineteenth and early twentieth centuries for it to be surveyed by archaeologists, who noted that the defences seemed to consist of two concentric rings.[298]

It has subsequently been recognized that, of these two concentric rings, only the outer is the actual *burh* built by Edward the Elder; the inner ring is the remains of the Bronze Age fort.[299] It should perhaps be noted that some landscape archaeologists have recently cast doubt on the Chipping Hill location as the site of the *burh*, but, given its strategic value, we await firm archaeological evidence to the contrary before deviating from the opinions of earlier generations of historians.

Very little of the *burh* remains to be seen. The *burh* roughly followed the circle suggested by the layout of these roads: Whitehorse Lane, Albert Road, Station Road, Avenue Road, and then the line of the Brain itself. However, beside the Brain, the two ramparts, Iron Age and Saxon, marched together,[300] and here the surviving remains give some impression of the scale of the fort. Here, where Chipping

Hill joins Collingwood Road, a new estate called Templemead stands atop the rampart. From this estate it can be seen that there is a considerable drop – about 10 m – down to the river valley below. The ramparts can also be seen from below in Earlsmead (where there is a house called 'Saxons'), curving away to follow the river bend. Further round in Collingwood Road is a Labour Party hall with an enormous car-park, and from this the profile of the rampart across at Templemead and on the other side of the railway lines can be seen. It is also possible to walk along the Brain on its western side for a further perspective.

Location: This is described above. Parking in the narrow estate roads of Earlsmead and Templemead may be awkward, and the Collingwood and Braintree Roads are busy through routes. There is some parking beside the station, which lies right in the middle of the *burh*. Visitors arriving by train will therefore be left in no doubt of the supremacy of the Age of Steam over the Saxon Age.

SITES IN OTHER COUNTIES

BUCKINGHAMSHIRE – Taplow

The name Taplow means 'Taeppa's burial-mound'; Taeppa may have been an early seventh-century warlord who carved out a territory in what is now south Buckinghamshire. It seems likely that Taeppa had political links with either or both the kingdom of the East Saxons and that of the East Angles (see discussion in Introduction), and the rich finds from his tumulus confirm cultural links. The barrow was excavated in 1883. Taeppa had been buried in a wooden coffin,[301] and buried with him were a garment embroidered with gold thread; a sword and wooden scabbard; a most beautiful gold buckle with gold thread; a sword and wooden scabbard; a most beautiful gold buckle ornamented with filigree work and inlaid with garnets; a pair of gilt bronze clasps; two iron knives; a hooped and staved bucket; a bronze bowl of Coptic workmanship; drinking horn mounts in silver gilt; a tub containing wooden and glass beakers; a spearhead; and a set of gaming counters. The finest of these pieces are now on show in the British Museum in the Early Medieval Gallery (see entry under London).

Taeppa's mound itself stands in the old churchyard next to Taplow Court. The old church was demolished in 1827. Both church and mound stood on a high spur of land, partially enramped and fortified, overlooking a strategic point in the Thames. The mound is 5 m high and 22 m in diameter, and in its quiet corner today presents a most striking relic of the turbulent politics of the East Saxon periphery during the early Anglo-Saxon period.

Location: Taplow lies beside the Thames opposite Maidenhead. It has its own railway station, beside the A4. From the M4, leave at junction 7 to get onto the A4. For pedestrians and motorists alike,

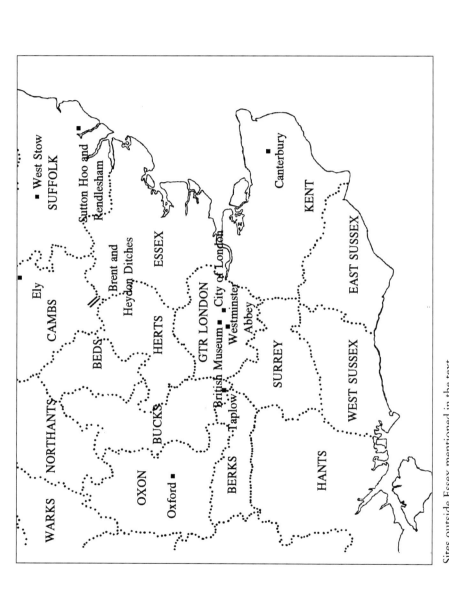

Sites outside Essex mentioned in the text

follow the A4 under the railway bridge towards Maidenhead then turn right into the B476. The old churchyard where the barrow is located is now in the grounds of Taplow Court; access is via the tradesmen's entrance to the left of the house.

CAMBRIDGESHIRE – Brent and Heydon Ditches

Cutting across the landscape of south Cambridgeshire is a network of linear earthworks described as an 'in-depth defence system'.[302] The date of these ditches and embankments is much in dispute, but it seems likely that they were erected early in the Anglo-Saxon period, and may be connected with Anglo-Saxon retrenchment after military defeat at the end of the fifth century. The dykes cut the main Roman road into East Anglia, and the two largest, Devil's Ditch and the Fleam Ditch, face the south-west, towards London, from which direction the threat presumably lay.

Of Essex interest are the two dykes further south, the Brent Ditch and the Heydon or Bran Ditch. These cut across two Roman roads leading out from the Saffron Walden/Great Chesterford region, which, as we now know, was a British statelet for some time after the Anglo-Saxon invasion (see entry for Saffron Walden). Both these earthworks faced outwards from the Walden statelet, the Brent Ditch cutting the road to the north, the Heydon Ditch the road to the west. Both dykes also cut the ancient Icknield Way as it curves round to the south-west from its long route through East Anglia.

Excavations at the Heydon Ditch in 1927 found fifty decapitated skeletons, some mutilated, buried in one spot. Six more bodies with marks of axe-cuts and spear-thrusts were found 200 m away; one was accompanied by a Saxon knife.[303] This has been interpreted as a massacre of Saxons attempting to attack the British heartland via the Icknield Way;[304] if this is correct then the forces from Walden may have been responsible for this devastating defeat – the killing of an entire boatload – of Saxon forces.

Location: The Brent Ditch cuts the A11 about 4 km beyond Great Chesterford, just across the Essex border. The earth bank, now overgrown with trees, can be clearly seen stretching away on either side of the road – it runs for about 2 km in both directions, and wellies are advisable as it can be very muddy. Heydon Ditch is now very difficult to find, however. It cuts the Icknield Way (the Essex boundary with Cambridgeshire until 1895), now a narrow, though motorable, lane running nearly parallel with the A505; this can be conveniently picked up at junction 10 of the M11. The section north of the Icknield Way is now a track leading to Heydon Grange, while the southern section has been designated part of the long-distance footpath the Harcamlow Way, which runs into Heydon village, just across the Essex border from Chrishall.

Ely

After the Battle of Maldon in 991 (see entry for Maldon), the body of Byrhtnoth, leader and hero of the Saxon side, was carried, headless, to Ely Cathedral for burial. He lay there undisturbed in the choir until 1769 when his tomb was opened during rebuilding work; his skeleton was indeed found to be headless, with a ball of wax where the skull should have been, and a deep wound to the collarbone. His body was re-interred in Bishop West's Chapel, which is in the south-east corner of the east end of the cathedral, where it lies today, buried below a small niche inscribed with his name, alongside other distinguished Anglo-Saxons of the tenth and eleventh centuries.[305]

Location: Ely lies on the A10, dominated by its magnificent cathedral, a landmark for miles around. The town is well used to visitors and provides all the usual facilities.

KENT – Canterbury

Here the first Apostle of Essex, Mellitus, was buried in 624 after serving as Archbishop of Canterbury. He was laid to rest in St Augustine's Abbey, and his original place of burial in the Anglo-Saxon abbey can still be seen.[306] At the ruins of the abbey, the layout of the original Anglo-Saxon monastery has been marked out among the remains and walls of the later buildings that occluded it. On the northern side of the nave is an excavated area, the *porticus* (side chapel) of St Gregory. Here a stone tablet marks the spot; 'St Mellitus consecrated First Bishop of the East Saxons 604 Third Archbishop of Canterbury 619–624 AD'. Mellitus lay alongside St Justus and St Lawrence; the spot is now protected by a wooden roof. Mellitus' body was later removed from this spot to a position of honour in the later medieval abbey. He lay immediately to the right of St Augustine's body at the far end of the church. The crypt chapel of

Our Lady is now all that is preserved of this building – Mellitus would have lain to the right and immediately above the stone altar.

Location: St Augustine's Abbey, Canterbury, is an English Heritage property, open every day. There is an admission charge. The abbey is on the east side of the city, beyond the walls; the entrance to the ruins is in Longport.

LONDON – Introduction

Late Roman London was a city already in decline, and by the fifth century may even have been largely abandoned, its walls too long to defend and its supply network collapsing. Whatever its economic position, it retained its topographical advantage – strategic oversight of the lower Thames at the lowest bridgeable point – and possibly a perceived status as 'central place'. This is difficult to prove archaeologically, but the flight of Britons to London after their defeat at the Battle of *Crecganford* (?Crayford) in 457 indicates that it still had some military significance. London may also have been the controlling power which organized the settlement at Mucking to guard the sea-approaches; there was also a ring of early Saxon settlement, some of a military nature, around London, notably at Mitcham, Croydon, Ham, Blackheath, Northolt, Staines and Shepperton.[307] There were various earthworks in the region both north and south of the Thames. The dating, use or re-use of these earthworks is problematic, but in all cases, the defences *face* London.

By the time Bede was writing, in the 730s he could, looking back over the previous century, refer to London as 'capital (of the East Saxons) . . . a trading centre for many nations who visit it by land and sea.'[308] The manner by which London was transformed from a sub-Roman citadel to East Saxon capital is very unclear, though it may have been a gradual process (see Introduction). Yet intensive archaeological work within the City walls has produced little evidence of Saxon occupation prior to the tenth century.[309] This difficulty was resolved after fresh place-name study and new archaeological evidence indicating that the 'trading centre for many nations' lay beyond the walls, along The Strand.

Substantial middle Saxon occupation has now been discovered in the area bounded by Charing Cross Road, High Holborn, Kingsway and The Strand, with further signs of occupation round Trafalgar

Square, along Fleet Street, and south of The Strand. In addition, the remains of a timber farm building have been discovered off Whitehall, and a waterfront embankment south of The Strand indicates waterborne trade.

This East Saxon *Lundenwic* dates back at least as far as the early seventh century – *Ludenwic* being the name more probably applied to this area as opposed to *Lundenburh*, meaning 'the walled city'.[310] In the face of Viking attacks and declining prosperity of Continental trading cities, *Lundenwic* seems to have declined in the ninth century and been abandoned in favour of *Lundenburh*, which once more came into its own.

Literary, topographic, and place-name evidence indicates that *Lundenburh* had been occupied, and was operating with certain specific functions, in the middle Saxon period, even though this is difficult to prove archaeologically. There were likely to have been two specific precincts within the walls in the seventh century, one royal, one ecclesiastical. The royal precinct was based at Aldermanbury, probably based on the gatehouse of the old Roman fort of Cripplegate (see entry under City of London), while the ecclesiastical precinct was further south at St Paul's (see entry under City of London).

As it grew in importance, the surrounding powers took a closer interest in London, and control of it was wrested from Essex. In 604 it was the Kentish king who organized the building of St Paul's, and in the 680s a Kentish reeve was in office in London to oversee the administration. In *c.* 623 the East Saxon Kings Saeward and Seaxred were killed in a battle with Wessex which may well have been a border dispute to the west of London. In 690 Ine, king of Wessex, referred to the bishop of London as 'my bishop'. However, amid these political fluctuations, it was the Mercians who were eventually able to take control of the London region and turn it into their chief port. This probably occurred in the eighth century, during the reign of the Mercian King Aethelbald (716–57), though the process of Mercian overlordship had begun earlier still. Between them, Aethelbald and his successor Offa made Mercia dominant throughout southern England, and the history of London thereafter was that of a Mercian city rather than of an East Saxon city. Later, Mercia was to collapse under the pressure of Viking assault, and it was the West Saxon hero Alfred who recovered London from the invaders and began its systematic re-planning. That fascinating story lies beyond the scope of this book.

The British Museum

The British Museum is one of the greatest museums in the world, covering the entire span of human history and culture displayed in over a hundred galleries in one of the finest neo-Classical buildings in the country. Much material from Essex has found its way to the British Museum, mainly deposited in the nineteenth century. From outside our period, there is important material from both prehistoric and Roman Essex in the Museum's collection. There is also, however, a wealth of East Saxon material on display, and fortunately for the visitor it is all assembled in a single gallery. This is Room 41, the Early Medieval Gallery, on the Museum's upper level. There is a pamphlet available for a small charge in the gallery explaining the displays, which trace the transition from the late Roman world to medieval Europe. The majority of the Essex material is, of course, from Mucking, its superb quality qualifying it for inclusion. The Broomfield Treasure can here be seen in its cultural context, with Sutton Hoo and Taplow artefacts close at hand for comparison of style.

The following material is on permanent display:

Case 29 (Germanic Glass AD 400–700). Two fifth- to sixth-century claw beakers, and a cone beaker of similar date. Numbers 2 and 8 are from Mucking, Number 2 being a claw beaker from Grave 843 and Number 8 being a cone beaker from Grave 924. Number 4 is a claw beaker from Grave 122 at Great Chesterford.

Case 31 (Early Medieval Weapons AD 400–1100). A sixth-century spear from Grave 51 at Great Chesterford.

Case 34 (The First Anglo-Saxon Settlers AD 400–500). There are several items from the fifth-century settlement of Mucking; Number 37 is the base of a pedestal pot from mid-century. Number 38 is a fragment from a bronze openwork buckle of a type issued to mercenary troops in late Roman times. Number 39 consists of fragments of four bowls.

Case 36 (Anglo-Saxon Farms and Villages). There are many items from East Saxon domestic contexts in this case, all from Mucking. Numbers 11–28 consist of domestic pottery (mainly fragmentary), dating from the fifth to seventh century. They include cooking pots, grain storage vessels, and the base of a strainer. There are also fifth- to sixth-century personal and domestic items; a bone comb backplate, a belt fitting, a glass beaker fragment, four brooches, and three silver coins known as *sceattas* from the reign of Kentish King Wihtred dating to about AD 690. Numbers 34–9 are domestic iron objects; a pin, two knives (one late Saxon), a pair of shears, a small razor, and a buckle loop. There are also five clay spindle-whorls, used in textile production and dating from the fifth to seventh century.

Case 37 (Anglo-Saxon Burials AD 400–700: Inhumations). Included on display here are grave goods from a sixth-century warrior burial, found in Grave 600 at Mucking. There is a bronze pommelled iron sword, with remains of its wooden scabbard bound with leather, a bronze-bound bucket, an iron shield boss, an iron knife blade, and an iron spearhead.

Case 38 (Anglo-Saxon Burials AD 400–700: Regional Identities). Number 14 consists of four brooches of the 'small-long' type, found at Great Chesterford and dating from the sixth century. Number 17 is a fifth-century gilt-bronze button brooch decorated with a face, found in Grave 99 at Mucking.

Case 44 (Broomfield and Caenby Burials). This case displays the remarkable treasures discovered at Broomfield in 1888 and 1894, the remains of a high-status burial from the early seventh century. There is a modern reconstruction of a wooden bucket, incorporating the original iron fittings, and part of a bronze bowl, in which were found two glass jars, also on display, and a cow's horn. There is an iron sword still in its scabbard, which can be compared with the nearby Taplow sword, and an iron tripod lamp which can be compared with a similar item found at Sutton Hoo, and a Frankish pot. The precious metal items, which also bear comparison with the Sutton Hoo finds, include pieces of a gold jewelled buckle incorporating garnet inlay, a gold sword fitting in the shape of a pyramid inlaid with garnets, and two silver gilt fittings from wooden cups.

Case 45 (Celtic Metalwork AD 700–1100). The extraordinary Steeple Bumpstead shrine boss is displayed in this case; this richly ornamented gilt-bronze piece was originally made in the eighth century in Ireland or Northumbria.

Case 47 (Anglo-Saxon Crafts and Commerce AD 700–1100). Number 53 is an inlaid copper-gilt brooch from Colchester.

Case 49 (Vikings in Britain & Ireland AD 800–1050: Raiders and Settlers). Number 23 is a gold ring from Thaxted dating from the tenth or eleventh century.

Case 50 (Vikings in Britain & Ireland AD 800–1100: Loot and Trade). Number 10 is a gold ring from Harwich.

CITY OF LONDON – All Hallows by the Tower

One of the few churches in the City to escape the Great Fire of London was All Hallows by the Tower, but it was hit and partially destroyed in the *Blitz*. As with other bombed churches, the destruction proved an opportunity to discover more about the church's history, and what was found takes us back to the seventh century, and the time when London was the capital of Essex. Indeed, it takes us further still into the past, for a tessellated pavement and parts of a second-century Roman house were found in the undercroft.

Anciently known as All Hallows, Barking, the church has long been recognized as a daughter church of Barking Abbey, founded on abbey land in the City in the seventh century, making it one of the City's most ancient ecclesiastical foundations.[311] Much of the Tower Hill area seems to have been owned by Barking Abbey; the tower itself was built on abbey land and while waiting for it to be completed, William lodged at Barking Abbey.

In the south-west corner of the nave stands a Saxon arch, built out of Roman tiles. This dates from about AD 675, so the church itself must have been stone-built from the start, and very large for a Saxon church; it extended the full length of the present church and was as wide as the central part of the nave between the pillars. The undercroft beneath is mainly fourteenth century, but elements of the Saxon church survive. The wall at the east end is Saxon, as are the walls supporting the west tower. There are also three Saxon coffins on display, and parts of a Saxon 'wheelhead' cross discovered incorporated in the fabric of the building in 1940.

Location: All Hallows Church stands in Byward Street, City of London. The main body of the church, including the Saxon arch, is normally kept open, but there are restricted opening hours for the undercroft. To check beforehand contact the church on 071 481 2928.

Cripplegate Fort

There is considerable circumstantial, though little archaeological, evidence that parts of the Roman Cripplegate fort in the City formed a royal precinct in the middle Saxon period.[312]

The Cripplegate fort stood in the north-west corner of *Londinium*, its axes marked by the present day Wood Street and Addle Street (both based on Roman roads). Addle Street (cf. Atheling meaning 'nobleman') follows the Roman road from the centre of the fort to what would have been the eastern gate, but instead of aligning itself with the Roman gateway it suddenly turns to emerge 30 m further north. The cause of the diversion is (or was) the medieval tenement of Aldermanbury, the 'fortified manor of the alderman', which stood squarely on the eastern gateway of the Cripplegate fort.

Aldermanbury possessed extensive privileges in the Middle Ages, and the tenement frontage still projects into the street named Aldermanbury exactly on the line of the gatehouse and wall. Medieval documents refer to Aldermanbury as the former site of a royal palace, used by successive kings until Edward the Confessor moved the royal seat to Westminster. After this removal, royal oversight of the City continued via an alderman, and thus the site acquired its name. In the 1120s the City's administration was moved 90 m south-east to the site of the present Guildhall, now known to be built on the remains of the City's amphitheatre.

Roman gatehouses also provided high status residences at York and Winchester, no doubt because of their easy defensibility; Continental examples are also known. A standing Roman strongpoint like a monumental gate would have been an obvious base for royal authority and, given its later royal associations, Aldermanbury may well have been the seat of East Saxon kings in London. Just south of the Aldermanbury estate stood its church of St Mary, Aldermanbury, destroyed in the *Blitz* and now laid out as a garden; a few pillars from the nave and some of the ruined walls have been left standing. St Mary's was almost entirely rebuilt by Wren, only the west tower being earlier.

Nearby stands the tower of St Alban, Wood Street. St Alban's was another Wren church destroyed in the *Blitz* and, but for its tower, it now lies buried beneath a dreary post-war streetscape. But destruction also revealed a hitherto hidden history. Excavated by Professor Grimes, the site revealed a double-celled church dated by him to the eighth century, though it may in fact be rather later. If eighth-century, St Alban's may well be linked to Offa, the founder or re-founder of St Alban's Abbey, Hertfordshire, and could well have formed the palace chapel of the royal precinct.[313]

Museum of London

The 'Dark Age of London' gallery of the Museum of London has a superb collection of Saxon artefacts, military and domestic, mainly from central London though there is some material from outer London boroughs. There is, however, nothing on display from east of the Lea, and disappointingly, the role of London as the capital of Essex is not mentioned. Neither is the fact that the East Saxon kingdom controlled London and its hinterland for at least two centuries during London's transition from Roman to Saxon city. The only overt link with Essex in the gallery is a replica of the Saxon arch from All Hallows by the Tower. That church's similarity to St Peter's-on-the-Wall, Bradwell-on-Sea, is noted in the information panel, which includes a photograph of St Peter's.

St Bride's Church, Fleet Street

St Bride's Church, Fleet Street, lies between the *Lundenwic* settlement along The Strand and the walls of Roman *Londinium*. Excavations in the crypt in 1940 by Professor W.F. Grimes revealed successive rebuilding on the church site since the Roman occupation. Parts of a Roman mosaic and pavement, a wall, ditch and burial chamber can be seen, and one suggestion is that the chuch began life as a Christian *martyrium* or shrine amid Roman London's extramural burial-grounds.[314] A Saxon building followed, with nave, chancel and apse. Professor Grimes was cautious about the dating of this church, but speculation soon arose that the building could be as old as the sixth century, perhaps founded by St Bridget herself at a locus of Irish settlement.[315] It was said that the church resembled the early church at Kildare, St Bridget's place of origin. If true, then this church was built when East Saxons were in control of London and its hinterland, thus falling within our field of interest. It is, however, now thought doubtful that the massive walls excavated could be so early as the sixth century, and while a continuous history through the Saxon conquest is possible, most scholars would now assign 'Saxon' St Bride's to the late rather than the early Saxon period.[316]

Location: St Bride's Church is in Fleet Street, in the City of London. The church and crypt are normally kept open, and as well as the Roman and Saxon architectural features in the crypt, there are cases displaying finds and relating the history of the church, or at least the optimistic early Saxon/St Bridget connection version discussed above.

St Paul's Cathedral

Unlike the legendary history surrounding the origins of Westminster Abbey (see entry below), the history of St Paul's Cathedral is well documented by a reliable source. The present St Paul's, Wren's great masterpiece, is the fifth cathedral to be built on the site; today the great building gives little hint of its humble origin as the missionary church for the East Saxons.

In 601 Pope Gregory the Great sent several clergymen to Britain to help St Augustine's mission. With the priests he sent a letter ordering the creation of an archbishopric based in London. (This proved impossible to carry out, and the archiepiscopal see is, of course, still based in Canterbury.) One of the priests was Mellitus, who received a famous letter from Gregory advising him how the pagan Saxon religion was to be dealt with: 'The temples of the idols among that people should on no account be destroyed. The idols are to be destroyed, but the temples themselves are to be aspersed with holy water, altars set up in them, and relics deposited there'.[317]

In 604 St Augustine consecrated Mellitus as the first bishop of the East Saxons, to be based in the capital, London. As Bede records,

> At this time Sabert, Ethelbert's nephew through his sister Ricula, ruled the province [of Essex] under the suzerainty of Ethelbert [king of Kent] . . . When this province [Essex] too had received the faith through the preaching of Mellitus, King Ethelbert built a church dedicated to the holy Apostle Paul in the city of London.[318]

The new faith had only a precarious hold in Essex for when Saberht died, his three sons reverted to paganism and Mellitus was driven into exile. The first Apostle of Essex was never to see London again, but became Archbishop of Canterbury in 619, dying in 624. It was to be a generation later before the East Saxons re-converted, in 653 at the behest of King Sigeberht II *Sanctus*. A second 'Apostle of Essex" arrived; this was St Cedd, who seems to have been based in Bradwell-on-Sea and East Tilbury (see separate entries) rather than London. However, the next bishop, Erkenwald, appointed *c.* 675, was very firmly based in London. He enlarged and rebuilt St Paul's and obtained papal privileges for it.[319] Founder of Barking and Chertsey Abbeys, his was the chief shrine of all the later cathedrals of St Paul's. The ecclesiastical precinct, which included St Paul's, St Martin within Ludgate, St Augustine's and St Gregory, may date from this period.

After Erkenwald's death, which occurred in 693, a vigorous cult sprang up, and even the horse-litter in which he travelled when ill was cut up into little pieces by the pious, who then took the pieces to cure the sick. Miracles were attributed to him. After his death at Barking there was supposed to have been a squabble for his body between Barking, Chertsey and St Paul's. The London faction eventually seized the body and made off with it towards the capital. However, a storm prevented them crossing the Roding at Ilford. At first this was interpreted as a sign against the London faction until, after prayers, the waters divided and, like the Israelites crossing the Red Sea, his supporters

> toke up the body with grete honour and reverence and by one assent they bare it though the path, the water standyng up on every syde; and the people not wetyng theyr feet and so they came to Stratforde and set down the bere in a fayre made of floures . . . And thus it pleased our Lorde for to multiplye myracles to the honour and worshyp of this holy Saynt.[320]

In a medieval hymn Erkenwald was described as 'the Light of London'. His body was moved in 1140 and 1148 to a spectacular and sumptuous shrine encrusted with precious stones, silver and gold, and placed at the high altar. In 1386 a middle English poem glorifying his life was written, probably to celebrate the fourteenth-century rebuilding of St Paul's. This extraordinary poem, replete with miracles, represented the pinnacle of Erkenwald's medieval cult.

Co-king of Essex during Erkenwald's episcopate was Saebbi, a devout and saintly man who died in 694. Bede records details of his life, and the miraculous events surrounding his burial. A stone sarcophagus prepared for his burial was found to be too short; when chiselled out further to the correct length, it was still too short. The embarrassed masons wondered whether to make another coffin or bend the body to make it fit, when it was found that 'miraculously' the body did fit, with plenty of room to spare. Saebbi was buried in St Paul's. In the medieval cathedral his body lay in a grey marble coffin on the north side of the choir, embellished with a Latin inscription.[321]

After the Great Fire of 1666, little survived of the old St Paul's. The tombs of Erkenwald and Saebbi were destroyed. The high altar, where the tomb of Erkenwald formerly stood, is now a memorial to the dead of the Second World War, and Erkenwald's only memorial is a stone tablet in the south aisle near the transept, listing the bishops of London; this list includes Mellitus, Cedd and Erkenwald. In the crypt, a memorial on the west side near Wren's Great Model reads, 'In pious memory of the famous dead whose remains lay buried in old St Paul's Cathedral or whose memorials perished in its destruction'. First on the list that follows is 'Sebba King of the East Saxons 677'.

Location: St Paul's stands at the top of Ludgate Hill in the City of London. The ambulatory including the high altar is open Monday to Friday, 10 a.m. to 4.15 p.m., Saturday, 11 a.m. to 4.15 p.m., and closed on Sunday. The crypt and treasury have the same opening hours, and there is a separate admission charge for both.

Westminster Abbey

The traditional foundation-legend of Westminster Abbey links it with Essex. However, such legends existed mainly to promote the antiquity of the church concerned; they were often supported by spurious charters and monkish tales of miraculous events. This is certainly the case with Westminster Abbey, whose real origins are unfortunately very obscure. The legends, however, claim that the abbey was founded by the East Saxon King Saberht about the year 616,

> who having imbraced Christianity, and being baptized by Melitus, Bishop of London, immediately (to show himself a Christian indeed) built a Church to the Honour of God and St Peter, on the West Side of the City of London, in a Place (which because it was overgrown with Thorns, and environed with Water) the Saxons caled Thorney.[322]

So far the tale is at least plausible. The London area was part of the East Saxon kingdom at the time, and, from Bede, we know that Saberht was converted by Mellitus in 604. Mellitus became bishop of the East Saxons and the Kentish paramount, King Ethelberht, had built for him the Cathedral of St Paul's in the City of London. St Peter's, Westminster, – the abbey – is not mentioned by Bede, but as one writer drily notes, 'there can be no doubt that the more important the [monastic] house became, the greater was the temptation to rival in antiquity the foundation stories of such houses'.[323]

So, for the credulous, there was more. As Mellitus was preparing to consecrate the abbey, St Peter himself appeared on a stormy night on the opposite shore. An astonished fisherman, one Edricus, was called upon to ferry the apostle across to Thorney. This being done, St Peter then consecrated the building himself in the presence of a heavenly host. On being ferried back across the river, St Peter charged Edricus to tell Mellitus what had happened so that Mellitus would not consecrate the church again. Edricus reminded St Peter that he required a reward for his service as ferryman, whereupon he gathered up a miraculous draught of salmon in his net. The one condition the apostle imposed was, conveniently, that from thenceforth London's fishermen should give to the abbey one tenth of all the salmon caught in the Thames.[324]

By tradition, Saberht is buried at Westminster Abbey, and his supposed tomb can still be seen. This monument lies in the south ambulatory (the walkway around the high altar and shrine of Edward the Confessor), between the tombs of Anne of Cleves and Richard II, facing the south transept. His simple tomb backs directly onto the high altar area: it was placed there in 1308, though whether Saberht was commemorated before that date is unknown. The tapering black marble tomb sits in a varnished recess, at the back of which are some fifteenth-century sculpted stone panels in the shape of quatrefoils enclosing flowers. A curt sign next to the monument informs us that 'according to medieval legend (Saberht) was the first founder of Westminster Abbey'.

In the high altar area itself, there is a remarkable painting of Saberht on the sedilia (the tall wooden panels behind the seats next to the high altar). The panel, which was painted in about 1300, shows Saberht as he was imagined to be by men of the Middle Ages; he is bearded, wears a red robe and a long cloak lined with white fur. His hands are gloved, and he holds a sceptre. The colours are fresh and glowing and it is hard to believe that 700 years separate us from the artist. The panel is on the south side of the high altar area (the presbytery), originally with three other paintings though two are now damaged. Saberht is the nearest to the high altar, and so a very close-up view is not possible – it is best seen from the seating area below the high altar steps.

There is also a later statue, thought to represent Saberht, in Henry V's chantry chapel. This ornate chapel, dating from the early fifteenth century, forms a kind of bridge over the eastern end of the ambulatory. There are two turret staircases on the north-west and south-west sides of the chapel leading directly into the area of the shrine of Edward the Confessor. Figures are sculpted on the exterior of the turrets, and one of them, high up on the north turret, is supposed to be Saberht. Here he is crowned and wears a full beard and a stern expression. He has a loose fitting robe and cloak, and in his left hand holds up a model of a building which is meant to represent Parliament. He looks directly down over the tomb of Edward the Confessor, and the Coronation Chair, and seems to guard the entrance to Henry V's tomb.

It should also be noted that the church of St Mary Magdalene at Great Burstead, better known for its magnificent medieval wall-paintings and its associations with the Pilgrim Fathers, is also said by some writers[325] to be Saberht's place of burial. However, no such claim appears to be expressed by the church itself, and the origin of the story is not clear. Earlier writers such as Morant (author of the *History and Antiquities of the County of Essex*, published 1763-8) make no mention of it.

There is no archaeological evidence for the founding of St Peter's, Westminster, during the East Saxon hegemony over London, though this does not make the story impossible. Most historians would, however, feel safer in ascribing the abbey's foundation to Offa, the Mercian king, after the area passed to Mercian control in the eighth century.[326] Its eleventh-century refoundation was the last great work of Edward the Confessor, for whom it became a deathbed obsession.

Location: Westminster Abbey lies at the heart of the City of Westminster. There is a charge to visit the 'Royal Chapels' area of Westminster Abbey, which is where the tomb, painting, and statue of Saberht all lie. Because of the crowds, there is also usually a one-way system operating round the ambulatory.

OXFORDSHIRE – Oxford

Oxford's Ashmolean Museum has one of the finest collections of Anglo-Saxon antiquities in the country. These are on display in Gallery 17, the E.T. Leeds Room, on the first floor. The finest East

Saxon piece is the beautiful and intricate gold bead set with crimson garnets and blue glass, in the form of a biconical cylinder. This large bead was part of a high-status female burial in Forest Gate (now in the London Borough of Newham), and dates from the first half of the seventh century. Stylistically it is paralleled by the workmanship in some of the finds from Broomfield, Sutton Hoo and Taplow.

Location: The Ashmolean Museum is in Beaumont Street, Oxford. Opening hours are Tuesday to Saturday, 10 a.m. to 4 p.m., Sunday, 2 p.m. to 4 p.m. Admission is free.

SUFFOLK – Rendlesham and Sutton Hoo

Today Rendlesham is a scattered parish in eastern Suffolk. The graceful flinty fourteenth-century church near the River Deben is still 'standing aloof with only trees for company'[327] just as Arthur Mee described it fifty years ago. In the seventh century, however, the church of Rendlesham served the royal court of the East Anglian kings which stood at this place. Here in a wooden church (long-since vanished), the East Saxon King Swithhelm (see Introduction) was baptized by Cedd some time between 653 and 664. Bede records this historic occasion, noting that the East Anglian King Ethelwald stood as godfather.[328] By tradition this was also the place where Swithhelm was buried.[329]

Today the church houses a small exhibition in a room over the porch. This room is reached by a precipitous staircase (not for the fainthearted!) to the right of the main door (as viewed from the inside), and the exhibition briefly outlines the story of the East Anglian kingdom and sites of interest nearby, most notably Sutton Hoo. At Sutton Hoo, overlooking the Deben, the windswept royal burial ground of the East Angles is being systematically excavated.

Location: Rendlesham church is normally kept open. From Woodbridge (the nearest station), follow the A12 northbound, turning off to the right on the A1152. Then follow signs for RAF Bentwaters, and travel until through the village of Eyke; about 1/2 km further on there is a minor road (signposted) to the left. Rendlesham church comes into view almost immediately. At Sutton Hoo nearby, the site of the royal tombs is on *private land*. There is, however, a signposted public footpath leading past the site. This lies off the

B1083. Follow the road from Woodbridge as for Rendlesham, but at the first roundabout take the B1083 rather than the A1152. There is a large parking area opposite the start of the footpath, where the Hollesley road joins the B1083. There are guided tours of the excavation at 2 p.m. and 3 p.m. on weekends and bank holidays between May and September.

West Stow

West Stow in Suffolk offers a unique opportunity to walk round a reconstructed Anglo-Saxon village. There are no Essex connections, but an outing to West Stow provides a fascinating look at the ways in which archaeological evidence has been interpreted. Excavations completed in 1972 revealed on this site an early Anglo-Saxon village consisting of about eighty timber buildings, huts and halls, ranging in date from the early fifth to the mid-seventh century. A number of these buildings have been reconstructed, as has some of the environment surrounding the Anglo-Saxon village. The reconstructions take into account varying interpretations of the structure of the buildings, including sunken-floored huts with and without floorboarding, huts with eaves and huts whose roofs reach to the ground, in ridge-tent style. The site is being developed so further buildings are going up and facilities are being improved.

Location: West Stow Anglo-Saxon village lies in West Stow Country Park, off the A1101 from Bury St Edmunds (the nearest station). Turn right off the A1101 at Flempton, go through the village of West Stow, turning left past the church. The Anglo-Saxon village is signposted, and lies about 1 km further on. It is open from 10 a.m. to 5 p.m. daily and there is an admission charge. Special events are sometimes held; for details phone 028484 718.

REFERENCES AND NOTES

NB. References to the four Royal Commission for Historic Monuments volumes for Essex (1916–23) have not been cited individually

1   Yorke, *passim*, Bailey (1988), *passim*
2   Myres, 209
3   *Anglo-Saxon Chronicle*, 12
4   Myres, 14
5   *Nennius*, xlvi
6   M.U. Jones (1980), 82–3
7   Drury and Rodwell (1980), 71
8   Dunnett, 143
9   Ibid.
10   Bassett (1989), 24
11   Ibid.
12   Ibid.
13   Drury and Rodwell (1980), 64
14   Bailey (1989), 121
15   Bassett (1989), 18
16   Ibid., 25
17   R. Huggins, *passim*
18   Bassett (1989), 20–1
19   Neale, 40
20   See map in Bailey (1989), 116
21   Ibid., 111
22   Ibid.
23   There are many variant spellings of the names of East Saxon kings. We have followed the spellings in Yorke
24   Yorke, 16
25   Bede, ii, 3

26   *Essex Landscape No. 1 – Historic Features*, 21
27   Rodwell (1980b), 11
28   Owen, 30
29   Yorke, 28
30   M. Alexander, 69
31   G. Morgan (1982), 85
32   Davis, 43, 106ff.
33   Yorke, 29
34   Ibid., 19
35   Bruce-Mitford, 93ff.
36   *VCH Essex*, ii, 329
37   Morris, 322
38   Bede, ii, 5
39   Yorke, 29
40   Ibid., 18
41   Ibid., 19
42   Wall, 152
43   Bede, iii, 30
44   Ibid., iv, 11
45   Yorke, 20
46   All etymological headnotes are from Reaney unless otherwise stated
47   Dunnett, 5
48   Reaney, 22
49   Morris, 100
50   J. Alexander, 200–2
51   Coates, 11–12
52   Drury (1980), 47–8
53   Drury and Rodwell (1979), *passim*; Drury and Rodwell (1980), 59–61
54   Laver, 183–5; Sherlock, 216
55   Bedwin, 13ff.
56   Drury and Rodwell (1979), *passim*
57   Drury and Rodwell (1979), n. 15, 150
58   *Anglo-Saxon Chronicle*, 164
59   Ibid., 165
60   Quoted in Down, 7
61   Pevsner, 56–7
62   Swanton, 26
63   Scarfe, 46
64   Rodwell (1980a), 118

65   Yorke, 2
66   Bede, iv, 7–10
67   Farmer, 137
68   Lockwood, 8
69   Ibid.
70   Ibid., 10–11
71   MacGowan, 35–8
72   Redknap, 359 and Hart, 32 for opposing views
73   Lockwood, 3
74   Edwards, 29
75   Lockwood, fig. 9
76   Pevsner, 63–4
77   Worley, 79
78   Bede, i, 30
79   Rudge, 140; also noted in G. Morgan (1982), 31–2
80   Reaney, 490
81   Gelling (1978), 106ff.
82   Bailey (1989), 121
83   Bassett (1989), 21–2
84   Pevsner, 81–2; Mee, *Essex*, 30
85   Box, 21–2; Worley, 11
86   Kimmis, 3
87   W.J.T. Smith, 28
88   Bede, iii, and Carter, *passim*, are the sources for this entry
89   Rivet and Smith, 434–5
90   Bede, iii, 22
91   Ibid.
92   Not in the base of the tower as claimed by G. Morgan (1982), 29
93   *VCH Essex*, i, 325
94   Bruce-Mitford, 65; Green, 76, 81–2, 135
95   Youngs, Clark and Barry, 134
96   Reaney, 243
97   Rodwell (1980b), 14
98   Reaney, 242
99   Reaney, 258
100   Bailey (1989), 121
101   *St Nicholas Church, Castle Hedingham*, 3
102   *St Nicholas Church, Castle Hedingham*, 2
103   Box, 94
104   Komlosy, 162

105   Steer, 1
106   Stenton, 545
107   *Anglo-Saxon Chronicle*, 79
108   *VCH Essex*, ii, 345
109   King, 143
110   *VCH Essex*, i, 292
111   Crummy (1984), 31–2
112   Crummy (1975), 16
113   *Anglo-Saxon Chronicle*, version A, (A Cottonian Fragment: British Museum, Cotton MS. Otho B xi, 2), 102
114   *Anglo Saxon Chronicle*, 103
115   Clarke, 17
116   Crummy (1980), 79
117   Drury (1982), 383
118   Ibid., 390
119   Ibid., 350
120   Ibid., 390–1
121   Ibid., 387–9
122   Kightly, 83
123   Drury (1982), 383–4
124   Kightly, 88–90
125   Stephenson, 409–13
126   Ibid., 411
127   Kightly, 83
128   Drury (1982), 383
129   Mee, *Essex*, 80
130   Gelling (1978), 119–23
131   Reaney, xxi, xxiii
132   Bassett (1989), 17–19, 21
133   Drury and Rodwell (1980), 61–4
134   Worley, 28
135   Bax, 184
136   Drury (1980), 130
137   Bassett (1989), 17–19
138   Drury and Rodwell (1980), 64
139   Drury (1980), 47
140   Drury and Rodwell (1980), 61
141   Gould, 233–4
142   Bede, iii, 22
143   G. Morgan (1969), 110
144   Loftus, 64–5

223 Gowing, 2–3
224 Rodwell (1980b), 10
225 Ibid., 11
226 Rodwell and Rodwell, 122
227 Ibid., 124–5
228 Drury and Rodwell (1980), 71, 73
229 Rodwell (1980b), 11
230 Pevsner, 298
231 Bassett (1989), 25
232 Bassett (1982), 14–15
233 Webster and Cherry, 141. For different views of the ditches' origin, see Chambers, 7 and Brooks, 183
234 Rowntree, 58–9
235 Reaney, xxviii
236 Ibid., 339
237 Blair, 97
238 Ibid., 106
239 Bede, iii, 30
240 Thurston and Attwater, iv, 52
241 Bax, 244
242 *The Essex Village Book*, 136
243 Arnold-Forster, ii, 386–7
244 *St Osyth's Priory*, 10–13
245 Smith and Wace, 168
246 Fearis, 157
247 Bax, 246
248 *Anglo-Saxon Chronicle*, version A, 86
249 Astbury, 202–3
250 A.C. Wright (1981b), 4
251 *VCH Essex*, i, 286, amplified in Gould, 232
252 Astbury, 202
253 Noted in Astbury, 204
254 *VCH Essex*, i, 287
255 Worley, 123
256 Scarfe, 66
257 There is a full description of the piece in Youngs, 146–7
258 Mee, *Essex*, 264
259 Parrott, 2
260 Pevsner, 344
261 Scarfe, 168
262 Laing, 163

263 Reaney, 302
264 Essex Journal, Vol. 22, No. 2
265 Ibid., 36
266 Gelling (1977), 8–10
267 Dean, *passim*
268 P.J. Huggins, *passim*
269 Dean, 3
270 Ibid., 4
271 Bax, 268
272 Mee, *Essex*, 282
273 Ibid., and *Waltham Abbey Historical Society Newsletter*, November 1991, 3
274 Higgs, 14
275 P.J. Huggins, 91
276 Ibid., 90
277 Reaney, 542
278 Mackay, i
279 Mee, *Essex*, 287
280 Mackay, iii
281 Starr (1985), *i*
282 Bascombe, 7–8; Eddy (1980), 9
283 T. Wright, ii, 742
284 Crummy, Hillam and Crossan, *passim*
285 Bede, iv, 11
286 Scarfe, 139, and *The Parish Church of St Peter and St Paul, West Mersea, passim*
287 Gelling (1978), 123
288 Eddy (1981), 9
289 Mee, *Essex*, 179
290 Astbury, 230
291 *Ibid.*
292 Mee, *Essex*, 290: Box, 121
293 Box, 121
294 Rodwell (1980b), 11
295 Gaimster, Margeson and Barry, 178–9
296 N. Smith, 84
297 *Anglo-Saxon Chronicle*, version A, 96
298 *VCH Essex*, i, 288
299 Petchey, 113
300 Ibid., 115
301 The account of the finds is from *VCH Bucks*, 200ff.

302   Kerr, 135
303   *VCH Cambs*, i, 310, Plate III
304   Morris, 100–2
305   Coatsworth, 279ff.
306   Sparks, 20
307   Dyson and Schofield, 289
308   Bede, ii, 3
309   Cowie and Whytehead, 706
310   Ibid., 707–8
311   Blewett and Drake, 4
312   Dyson and Schofield, 307–8
313   Weinreb and Hibbert, 688
314   D. Morgan, 6
315   Weinreb and Hibbert, 698
316   Brooke and Keir, 136–8, 139–40
317   Bede, i, 30
318   Ibid., ii, 3
319   *St Erkenwald*, 19
320   From the *Golden Legend*, quoted in Fry, 6
321   Stow, iii, 157
322   Ibid., vi
323   *VCH London*, i, 90
324   Brayley, i, 5–6
325   Box, 48
326   Brooke and Keir, 18
327   Mee, *Suffolk*, 327
328   Bede, iii, 22
329   Wall, 152

BIBLIOGRAPHY

Alexander, J.A. et al., 'Ambresbury Banks, an Iron Age Camp in Epping Forest, Essex' in *Essex Archaeology and History*, Vol. 10 (1978)

Alexander, Marc, *British Folklore, Myths and Legends*, Weidenfeld and Nicolson (1982)

Anglo-Saxon Chronicle, tr. G.N. Garmonsway, J.M. Dent (1972)

Arnold-Foster, Frances, *Studies in Church Dedications* (1899)

Astbury, A.K., *Estuary*, Carnforth Press (1980)

Bailey, Keith, 'East Saxon Kings – Some Further Observations' in *Essex Journal*, Vol. 22, No. 3 (1988)

——, 'The Middle Saxons' in *The Origins of Anglo-Saxon Kingdoms*, Leicester, Leicester University Press (1989)

Bartlett, Richard, 'Excavations at Harlow Temple 1985–87' in *Essex Journal*, Vol. 23, No. 1 (1988)

Bascombe, K.N., 'Congress Archaeological Symposium 1978' in *Essex Journal*, Vol. 14, No. 1 (1979)

Bassett, Steven, *Saffron Walden to AD 1300*, Chelmsford Archaeological Trust (1982)

——, 'In Search of the Origins of Anglo-Saxon Kingdoms' in *The Origins of Anglo-Saxon Kingdoms*, Leicester, Leicester University Press (1989)

Bax, Clifford, *Highways and Byways in Essex*, Macmillan (1939)

Bede, *A History of the English Church and People*, tr. Leo Sherley-Price, Penguin (1968)

Bedwin, Owen, 'Asheldham Camp – an early Iron Age hill fort: the 1985 excavations' in *Essex Archaeology and History*, Vol. 22 (1991)

Benton, Philip, *The History of Rochford Hundred*, Rochford (1867–8)

Blair, John, 'Frithuwold's Kingdom and the Origins of Surrey' in *The Origins of Anglo-Saxon Kingdoms*, Leicester, Leicester University Press (1989)

Blake, N.F., 'The Genesis of The Battle of Maldon' in *Anglo-Saxon England*, Vol. 7 (1978)

Blewett, Revd Philip, and Drake, Jane (eds.), *All Hallows by the Tower*, Andover, Pitkin Pictorials (1990)

Box, K. Dixon, *24 Essex Churches*, Essex Countryside/Anglian Publications (1965)

Brayley, Edward W., *The History and Antiquities of the Abbey Church of St Peter, Westminster* (1818)

Brooke, Christopher N.L., and Keir, Gillian, *London 800–1216: The Shaping of a City*, Secker and Warburg (1975)

Brooks, Howard, 'Excavations at Fairycroft House, Saffron Walden, 1990' in *Essex Archaeology and History*, Vol. 22 (1991)

Bruce-Mitford, R.L.S., *The Sutton Hoo Ship-Burial*, British Museum Publications (1979)

Butler's Lives of the Saints, eds. Herbert Thurston S.J. and Donald Attwater, Tunbridge Wells, Burns & Oates (1956)

Carter, H. Malcolm, *The Fort of Othona and the Chapel of St Peter-on-the-Wall, Bradwell-on-Sea, Essex*, St Peter's Chapel Committee (1987)

Catton, Jonathan P.J., 'E.T.-B.C. A Popular View: Archaeological Notes on the Parish of East Tilbury' in *Panorama*, No. 26, Thurrock Local History Society (1984)

Chambers, Wilfred, 'The Mystery of the Battle Ditches' in *Saffron Walden Historical & Archaeological Society Occasional Papers*, No. 1 (1968)

Christie, Hakon, Olsen, Olaf, and Taylor, H.M., 'The Wooden Church of St Andrew at Greenstead, Essex' in *The Antiquaries Journal*, Vol. LIX (1979)

Christy, Miller, 'Mound at Harlow' in *Essex Review*, Vol. XXXVI, No. 143 (1927)

Clarke, Joan and David, *Camulodunum*, Ginn and Company (1971)

Coates, Richard, *Linguistic History of Early Sussex*, University of Sussex (1983)

Coatsworth, Elizabeth, 'Byrhtnoth's Tomb' in *The Battle of Maldon AD 991* (D. Scragg (ed.)), Oxford, Basil Blackwell (1981)

Cocks, Heather and Hardie, Colin, *St Giles, Great Hallingbury* (1990)

Cowie, Robert and Whytehead, Robert, '*Lundenwic*: The Archaeological Evidence for Middle Saxon London' in *Antiquity*, Vol. 63, No. 24 (1989)

Crummy, Philip, *Not Only a Matter of Time*, Colchester Excavation Committee (1975)

——, 'Colchester between the Roman and Norman Conquests' in *Archaeology in Essex to AD 1500*, CBA Research Report No. 34 (1980)

——, *In Search of Colchester's Past*, Colchester Archaeological Trust (1984)

Crummy, Philip, Hillam, Jennifer, and Crossan, Carl, 'Mersea Island: The Anglo-Saxon Causeway' in *Essex Archaeology and History*, Vol. 14 (1982)

Davis, K. Rutherford, *Britons and Saxons – The Chiltern Region 400–700*, Chichester, Phillimore (1982)

Dean, Dinah, *The Legend of the Miraculous Cross of Waltham*, Waltham Abbey Historical Society (1975)

Down, Jonathan, 'The Problem of the Location of Assandun' in *Essex Journal*, Vol. 22, No. 1 (1987)

Drury, P.J. 'The Early and Middle Phases of the Iron Age in Essex' in *Archaeology in Essex to AD 1500*, CBA Research Report No. 34 (1980)

——, 'Aspects of the Origins and Development of Colchester Castle' in *The Archaeological Journal*, Vol. 139 (1982)

Drury, P.J. and Rodwell, Warwick, 'Investigations at Asheldham, Essex' in *The Antiquaries Journal*, Vol. LVIII (1979)

——, 'Settlement in the later Iron Age and Roman periods' in *Archaeology in Essex to AD 1500*, CBA Research Report No. 34 (1980)

Dunnett, Rosalind, *The Trinovantes*, Duckworth (1975)

Dyson, Tony and Schofield, John, 'Saxon London' in *Anglo-Saxon Towns in Southern England*, Chichester, Phillimore (1984)

Eddy, M.R. 'Excavations in Essex, 1978' in *Essex Journal*, Vol. 15, No. 1 (1980)

——. 'Excavations in Essex, 1979' in *Essex Journal*, Vol. 16, No. 1 (1981)

Edwards, A.C., *A History of Essex*, Chichester, Phillimore (1978)

Essex Landscape No. 1 – Historic Features, Essex County Council (1979)

The Essex Village Book, The Federation of Essex Women's Institutes (1988)

Farmer, D., *The Oxford Dictionary of Saints*, Oxford, Oxford University Press (1982)

Fearis, W. Hart, 'Fundamental Errors in the Article of St Osyth published in the Dictionary of Christian Biography' in *Essex Review*, Vol. LXI, No. 243 (1952)

Fry, Katharine, *History of the Parishes of East and West Ham* (1888)

Gaimster, David, R.M., Margeson, Sue, and Barry, Terry, 'Medieval Britain in 1988' in *Medieval Archaeology*, Vol. 33 (1989)

Gelling, Margaret, 'Latin Loan-Words in Old English Place-Names' in *Anglo-Saxon England*, Vol. 6 (1977)

——, *Signposts to the Past*, Dent (1978)

Glennie, Donald, *Our Town*, Civic Publications, Southend-on-Sea (1947)

Gould, I. Chalkley, 'Traces of Saxons and Danes in the Earthworks of Essex' in *Archaeological Journal*, Vol. LXIV (1907)

Gowing, Ellis N., *The Story of Prittlewell Church*, Prittlewell Parochial Church Council (1932)

Green, Charles, *Sutton Hoo*, Merlin Press (1963)

A Guide to Harlowbury Chapel, Harlow, Friends of Harlowbury Chapel (198?)

Hart, Cyril, *The Early Charters of Barking Abbey*, Benham (1953)

Hewett, Cecil A. and Taylor, H.M., 'The Chapel at Harlowbury, Harlow, Essex' in *Medieval Archaeology*, Vol. 23 (1979)

Higgs, Eric, *Waltham Abbey*, Andover, Pitkin Pictorials (1979)

Huggins, P.J., 'The Excavation of an 11th-century Viking Hall and 14th-century Rooms at Waltham Abbey, Essex, 1969–71' in *Medieval Archaeology*, Vol. 20 (1976)

Huggins, Rhona, 'The Significance of the Place-Name *Wealdham*' in *Medieval Archaeology*, Vol. 19 (1975)

Jones, M.U., 'Ancient Landscape Palimpsest at Mucking' in *Essex Archaeology and History*, Vol. 5 (Third Series) (1973)

——, 'An Early Saxon Landscape at Mucking, Essex' in *British Archaeological Report*, No. 6 (1974)

——, 'Excavations at Mucking, Essex: A Second Interim Report' in *The Antiquaries Journal*, Vol. LIV, Part II (1975)

——, 'Mucking and the Early Saxon Rural Settlement in Essex' in *Archaeology in Essex to AD 1500*, CBA Research Report No. 34 (1980)

Jones, W.T., 'A Note on Romano-British Pottery from East Tilbury' in *Panorama*, No. 21, Thurrock Local History Society (1977–8)

Judson, Eileen M., *History and Environment of Little Bardfield* (1981)

Kerr, Nigel and Mary, *A Guide to Anglo-Saxon Sites*, Granada (1982)

Kightly, Charles, *Folk Heroes of Britain*, Thames & Hudson (1984)

Kimmis, Jim, *Essex Church Dedications*, Colchester, E.L.M. (1981)

King, David J. Cathcart, *Castellarium Anglicanum*, Vol. 1, New York, Kraus (1983)

Komlosy, Revd F.F., 'The Parish and Church of Chickney' in *Essex Review*, Vol. XXXVI, No. 144 (1927)

Laking, Lloyd and Jennifer, *A Guide to the Dark Age Remains in Britain*, Constable (1979)

Laver, P.G., '*Sunecastre*, or the Camp at Asheldham' in *Transactions of the Essex Archaeological Society*, New Series, Vol. XIX (1930)

Lockwood, H.H., 'Where was the First Barking Abbey?' in *Barking & District Historical Society Transactions*, New Series, No. 1 (1986)

Loftus, E.A., 'Cameos of Local History' in *Panorama*, No. 26, Thurrock Local History Society (1984)

MacGowan, Kenneth, 'Saxon Timber Structures from the Barking Abbey Excavations 1985–1986' in *Essex Journal*, Vol. 22, No. 2 (1987)

Mackay, John, *Wendens Ambo Church Essex* (1987)

The Maldon Burh Jigsaw, Maldon Archaeological Group (1986)

Mee, Arthur, *Suffolk (The King's England series)*, Sevenoaks, Hodder & Stoughton (1941)

——, *Essex (The King's England series)*, Sevenoaks, Hodder & Stoughton (1966)

Morant, Philip, *The History and Antiquities of the County of Essex*, (1763–8)

Morgan, Dewi, *St Bride's Church, Fleet Street in the City of London*, Saint Bride Restoration Fund (1987)

Morgan, Glyn, *Forgotten Thameside*, Letchworth Printers (1969)

——, *Secret Essex*, Romford, Ian Henry (1982)

Morris, John, *The Age of Arthur*, Chichester, Phillimore (1977)

Myres, J.N.L., *The English Settlements*, Oxford, Oxford University Press (1986)

Neale, Kenneth, *Essex in History*, Chichester, Phillimore (1977)

Nennius (British History and the Welsh Annals), ed. J. Morris, Chichester, Phillimore (1980)

Owen, Gale R., *Rites and Religions of the Anglo-Saxons*, Newton Abbot, David & Charles (1981)

The Parish Church of St Edmund and St Mary, Ingatestone, Ingatestone (1983)

The Parish Church of St Mary and All Saints, Stambridge, Stambridge (1988)

The Parish Church of St Peter and St Paul, West Mersea, West Mersea (1984)

Parrott, Revd David, *Parish Church of Saint Mary the Virgin*, Strethall (1990)

Petchey, M.R., 'The Archaeology of Medieval Essex Towns' in *Archaeology in Essex to AD 1500*, CBA Research Report No. 34 (1980)

Petty, George R. and Susan, 'Geology and the Battle of Maldon' in *Speculum*, Vol. 51 (1976)

Pevsner, Niklaus, *Essex (The Buildings of England series)*, Penguin (1954)

Pollitt, William, *A History of Prittlewell*, Southend-on-Sea Museums Service (Handbook No. 9) (1968)

Powell, W. Raymond, 'The Medieval Hospitals at East Tilbury and West Tilbury and Henry VIII's Forts' in *Essex Archaeology and History*, Vol. 19 (Third Series) (1988)

Priddy, Deborah (ed.), 'Excavations in Essex' in *Essex Archaeology and History*, Vol. 13 (1981)

——, 'Excavations in Essex' in *Essex Archaeology and History*, Vol. 17 (1986)

Reaney, P.H., *The Place-Names of Essex*, Cambridge, Cambridge University Press (1935)

Redknap, Mark, 'The Saxon Pottery from Barking Abbey: Part I, local wares' in *London Archaeology*, Vol. 6, No. 13 (1991)

Rivet, A.L.F., and Smith, Colin, *The Place-Names of Roman Britain*, Guildford, Princeton University Press (1979)

Rodwell, Warwick, *Under Hadstock Church*, Hadstock (1974)

——, 'The Archaeological Investigation of Hadstock Church, Essex: An Interim Report' in *The Antiquaries Journal*, Vol. LVI (1976)

——, 'Ecclesiastical Sites and Structures in Essex' in *Archaeology in Essex to AD 1500*, CBA Research Report No. 34 (1980)

——, 'Church Archaeology' in *A Guide to Essex Churches*, Essex Churches Support Trust (1980)

Rodwell, Warwick and Kirsty, 'The Roman Villa at Rivenhall, Essex: An Interim Report' in *Britannia*, Vol. 4 (1974)

Rowntree, C. Brightwen, 'Legacies of the Ice Age in Essex' in *Essex Countryside*, Vol. 2, No. 6 (1954)

Royal Commission on Historical Monuments, London, Vol. I, HMSO (1924)

Rudge, Lilian, 'Pagan Stones and Essex Churches' in *Essex Countryside*, Vol. 5, No. 19 (1957)

'St Erkenwald' in *The Owl and the Nightingale/Cleanness/St Erkenwald*, tr. Brian Stone, Penguin (1971)

St Nicholas Church, Castle Hedingham (1986)

St Osyth's Priory, Derby, English Life Publications (1986)

Saunders, A., 'Chapel – Hospital – Blockhouse?' in *Panorama*, No. 13, Thurrock Local History Society (1970)

Scarfe, Norman, *Essex (Shell Guide)*, Faber (1968)

Scragg, D.G., *The Battle of Maldon*, Manchester, Manchester University Press (1981)

Sherlock, J.W., 'The Early Iron Age Site at Asheldham' in *Essex Review*, Vol. LV, No. 220 (1946)

A Short Look at a Saxon Church (St Katherine's Church, Little Bardfield) n.d.

Smith, Nicola, 'England's Oldest House?' in *Country Life*, Vol. CLXXXIII, No. 35 (1989)

Smith, William and Wace, Henry, *A Dictionary of Christian Biography* (1887)

Smith, William J.T., 'Finds at Boreham Church' in *Essex Journal*, Vol. 14, No. 2 (1979)

Sparks, Margaret, *St Augustine's Abbey, Canterbury, Kent*, English Heritage (1990)

Starr, Christopher, *St Mary's Old Church, West Bergholt*, Redundant Churches Fund (1985)

Steer, Francis W., *Chickney St Mary*, Redundant Churches Fund (1975)

Stenton, F.M., *Anglo-Saxon England*, Oxford, Oxford University Press (1971)

Stephenson D., 'The Colchester Chronicle and the Early History of Colchester Castle: A Preliminary Analysis' in Drury, 1982 (see above)

Stow, John, *A Survey of the Cities of London and Westminster* (1720)

Swanton, M.J., 'Dane-Skins: Excoriation in Early England' in *Folklore*, Vol. 87, The Folklore Society (1976)

Tyler, Susan, 'The Anglo-Saxon Cemetery at Prittlewell, Essex; an analysis of the grave goods' in *Essex Archaeology and History*, Vol. 19 (1988)

Victoria County History of Buckinghamshire, Vol. i (1905)

Victoria County History of Cambridgeshire and Isle of Ely, Vol. i (1938)

Victoria County History of Essex, Vol. i (1903)

Victoria County History of Essex, Vol. ii (1907)

Victoria County History of Essex, Vol. iii (1963)

Victoria County History of London, Vol. i (1909)

Wall, J. Charles, *The Tombs of the Kings of England* (1891)

Waltham Abbey Historical Society Newsletter, November 1991

Webster, Leslie E. and Cherry, John, 'Medieval Britain in 1972' in *Medieval Archaeology*, Vol. 17 (1973)

Weinreb, Ben and Hibbert, Christopher, *The London Encyclopaedia*, Macmillan (1983)

Worley, G., *Essex: A Dictionary of the County mainly Ecclesiological*, Bell (1915)

Wright, A.C., *South-east Essex in the Danish and Norman Periods*, Southend-on-Sea Museums Service (Handbook No. 20) (1981)

——, *South-east Essex in the Saxon Period*, Southend-on-Sea Museums Service (Handbook No. 21) (1981)

Wright, Thomas, *The History and Topography of the County of Essex* (1836)

Yorke, Barbara, 'The Kingdom of the East Saxons' in *Anglo-Saxon England*, Vol. 14 (1985)

Youngs, Susan (ed.), *'The Work of Angels' – Masterpieces of Celtic Metalwork, 6th–9th centuries* AD, British Museum Publications (1989)

Youngs, Susan, Clark, John, and Barry, Terry, 'Medieval Britain in 1985' in *Medieval Archaeology*, Vol. 30 (1986)